Mining for wisdom

Mining for wisdom

A twenty-eight-day devotional based on the book of Job

Derek Thomas

EVANGELICAL PRESS

EVANGELICAL PRESS
Faverdale North Industrial Estate, Darlington, DL3 0PH,
England

Evangelical Press USA
P. O. Box 84, Auburn, MA 01501, USA

e-mail: sales@evangelicalpress.org
web: http://www.evangelicalpress.org

First published 2002

British Library Cataloguing in Publication Data available

ISBN 0 85234 531 3

Printed and bound in Great Britain by Creative Print and
Design Wales, Ebbw Vale, South Wales.

To
Anne and Andrea

'*I know you are enduring patiently and bearing up for my name's sake, and you have not grown weary*'
(Rev. 2:3).

Contents

Preface

I have been living in the book of Job for the past ten years or more. In some ways, it has proved both a luxury and an obsession. In part, it became the material for a doctoral dissertation — but fear not, this is not what this book is about!

My wife refers to this book as 'The Sequel!' Evangelical Press were kind enough to publish a study of mine on the fifteen Ascent Psalms (120 – 134) called *Making the Most of Your Devotional Life* (2001). Many received it well and urged enthusiastically that I consider doing another title along the same lines. One reviewer took great exception to the notion that I urged upon my readers that there is such a thing as a *reformed* spirituality. I understand the reaction, partly because it suggests that only reformed Christians know anything about true spirituality. I do *not* believe that. What I meant was that our theology governs and affects everything, including the way we approach spirituality. In essence, what I said then I repeat now: reformed spirituality is a response to God's Word, written and expounded. In particular, I wrote these words:

> Spirituality must be biblically realistic. Realistic, that is, about what can and cannot be achieved in this world as far as our conformity to Christ and his image is concerned; what we generally refer to as sanctification. Realistic? Yes, because unreality abounds in this area.

Recognition that we live in a battlefield, surrounded within and without by implacable enemies bent on our destruction, is vital to our world view as Christians.[1]

I stand by those words more than ever. In Job, we deal with life at its worst, when expectations and dreams are shattered. We are dealing with raw nerves and any hint of unreality about what we may expect in following Jesus deserves the cynicism that follows. Sadly, the church is riddled with such false expectations and we are in need of help in coping with pain as much now as ever. When C. S. Lewis wrote *The Problem of Pain* (in 1940 when Europe was torn apart by war) he was addressing an issue that had been a 'problem' since Eden and remains so.

Lewis daringly suggested that God's moral judgement must differ from ours 'not as *white* from *black* but as a perfect circle from a child's first attempt to draw a wheel'. We want 'not so much a Father but a grandfather in heaven', a God 'who said of anything we happened to like doing, "What does it matter so long as they are contented?"' But love is not mere kindness. 'Kindness cares not whether its object becomes good or bad, provided only that it escapes suffering', while love 'would rather see [the loved ones] suffer much than be happy in contemptible and estranging modes'.

Whatever we may make of Lewis' precise line of argument, and some will disagree with it in parts, the main point is well taken: pain can teach us something about God — that we do not understand him as well as we think we do. Admitting such is not a retreat into a pessimism about ever knowing God at all; rather, it is to admit that there are depths to God that are 'past finding out'. To admit this is to approach the essence of true discipleship — at least, that is my conviction as to what the book of Job is essentially about.

I have decided to lay out the 'lessons' over twenty-eight days, which neatly covers four weeks — a month, more or less, in Job! I have suggested some verses from Job that can be read each day. It would be ideal if readers would follow this plan and assign some time to prayer and meditation on these passages before reading the explanation that follows.

Some will read this volume because they are suffering terribly and need all the help they can get. Some may have struggled with pain for a while and need to take stock on where they are in their relationship with God. Some may be strangers to pain — although no one is really that estranged — and may approach this book 'academically'. The latter may find the 'For your journal' sections at the end of each day's reading irritating and may decide to pass them by. Let me, then, say a word in favour of keeping a journal.

Keeping a journal has become faddish. Book stores all carry journals from cheap and tawdry to leather-bound deluxe editions. Their purpose? To write down (and therefore keep accountable) ideas, lessons, goals, even failures that each day has brought. I teach a course at the seminary where I reside (Reformed Theological Seminary, Jackson, Mississippi) on 'Spiritual Disciplines' and assign as a course requirement the keeping of a journal for what is approximately three months (the duration of a semester). Reading them (and I must have read several hundred) can be amusing, sometimes deeply disappointing, often inspiring and (yes!), frequently breathtaking. I have found students to be so honest in their struggles and concerns that I have had to impose a 'I promise not to tell' clause in the syllabus!

As a child I kept diaries. Recently, I have discovered the joys of keeping a journal myself (partly, by observing that the Puritans kept journals of their spiritual experiences). I recommend the chapter on 'journaling' in Don Whitney's *Spiritual Disciplines for the Christian Life* for those who remain sceptical. Believe me, making such a record can keep you accountable and spiritually sensitive in a way that few other things can. However, you may still not want to do so and I trust this book will serve to instruct without it.

Many people help in the course of writing a book, not least the editorial staff of Evangelical Press, for whom I am profoundly grateful. Others need mentioning by name. My former Thornwell assistant and friend, Marshall Brown, was always an encourager to me. He has now moved on to more rewarding ministries at the University of Alabama as a Reformed University Fellowship minister of the Presbyterian Church in America. My secretary, Ruth Bennett (actually I share her with several others!), was kind enough to proof-read this manuscript in several of its stages of production. Margaret Tohill urged me to publish the material after hearing me preach a series of sermons on Job at First Presbyterian Church, Jackson, where I serve (in addition to my work at the seminary) as the Minister of Teaching. Margaret has known, to a degree more than most, of the pain which Job's story tells. Though I have no doubt she, and her husband Jim, know the dereliction of which Job chapter 3 speaks, their outward faith is there for everyone to observe. I am also deeply thankful to the Executive Board of Reformed Theological Seminary and to its newly appointed President, Dr Ric Cannada, for their generosity in granting me a sabbatical in order to devote some time to these writing projects. I must say that I have often felt deeply guilty in spending time on that which I love so much.

I am grateful, too, to my friend (and boss!) Ligon Duncan, the senior minister at First Presbyterian Church, for the opportunities he has given to serve among these dear people. Ligon has been a joy to work with and for, a source of untiring enthusiasm and zeal for my paltry contributions, and a razor-sharp mind that I have plundered on too many occasions to recall.

I have preached on Job twice: once at Stranmillis Evangelical Presbyterian Church in the late eighties, and more recently at First Presbyterian Church. On both occasions, I felt when reaching the end that I was ready to begin the study again, having grasped a little more of what the book was about. There are depths that still elude me.

As I wrote these pages, Anne Gordon and her daughter Andrea frequently came into my mind. When I first went to Belfast, Northern Ireland, in 1979, with wide-eyed zeal for ministry, Anne's struggles with a daughter suffering from an acute and life-threatening condition forced me to think about suffering in a way that I cannot now fully relate. Anne has borne unimaginably difficult trials over the past twenty-five years. As a young minister, unknowingly to her I'm sure, she deeply influenced my understanding of true discipleship in the face of overwhelming odds. It is to these two, Anne and Andrea, that I dedicate this book.

Derek Thomas
December 2002

Day 1
Give me wisdom

Job 1

'There was a man in the land of Uz whose name was Job, and that man was blameless and upright, one who feared God and turned away from evil' (Job 1:1).

Suggested reading: Job 1:1-5

Joseph Caryl, a seventeenth-century Congregationalist minister in London, gave 424 lectures on the book of Job to his congregation. It took him over twenty-four years! At the conclusion, he confessed frankly that certain parts of it still baffled him!

The book of Job can be intimidating reading. Perhaps you have read it, and wondered, *what does it mean?*

People sometimes turn to the book of Job when they are hurting, in the hope of finding answers to their many questions. Surely, of all the books in the Bible, this one ought to answer those deep questions that begin with, 'Why?' or 'What?' or 'When?'

Why does God allow suffering?
Why does it have to be me?
What is the purpose of it all?
When is it going to end?

It is certainly tempting to think that the book of Job will answer such questions. After all, it is not difficult to imagine that God might provide us with at least one book in the Bible that addresses specifically such cries from the heart as these.

The problem is, however, that many have concluded that the book of Job does not answer the questions posed by pain and suffering. Some Christians have come away confused and baffled by the arguments made in this lengthy story.

So, what is this book about? It has something to do with trouble, but does it answer the deep questions about the purpose of everything? Is the book of Job God's 'Answer Book' for Christians troubled by perplexing questions about life and how hard it can sometimes be? The answer to that question is both 'Yes' and 'No'! The book of Job is designed to tell us something about suffering and God's part in it; but not quite in the way we might expect.

There is perhaps no greater story in the Bible than this one: the story of Job and his trial. Everyone can relate to the account of his pain to some degree. We may not feel that life has treated us quite as harshly; and there again, we may think that it has. Nevertheless, many of us have discovered that when life turns sour, we turn to the Scriptures for help. We remember that one of its books is given over entirely to answering the questions that arise from those dark places of tenderness and discomfort. We have begun to read the opening chapters with their description of Job's sudden collapse. It looks promising, but those endless speeches from Job's friends — what are we to make of them?

The book of Job reads like an enigma — a puzzle that only the initiated can solve. And most of us cannot find the key!

But wait a minute! Doesn't the book of James give us a key when it says that Job was a *patient* man (James 5:11, AV)?

Not really! We only have to turn to chapter 3, where Job is expressing a desire that he had never been born, to discover that 'patience' isn't the first word we would think of when describing Job. When we read the book of Job we get the distinct impression that though Job was many things, patient was not one of them.

Does that mean that James is in error, then? Not at all! The translation is the problem. By 'patient', James does not mean something passive and inactive; rather, the word he uses conveys a more active idea like perseverance, stickability, and the will to keep going when all the lights go out. That's why some translations use the words 'perseverance', or 'steadfastness'. Job *persevered*, even in his darkest moments. He kept going even when he paused to complain! Even when he was angry, he never lost sight of God. He held on to him tenaciously, even when he was saying things that, later, he would regret.

So, what is the message of the book of Job? There is a 'marker' in the opening verse that helps us understand what kind of book this is. We read that Job 'feared God' (1:1). Later, in Job 28:28, we learn that to fear God is an act of 'wisdom'.

The book of Job is about wisdom — the wisdom of God, not the wisdom of man.

Along with Proverbs and Ecclesiastes, Job belongs to the 'wisdom literature' of the Bible. But what does that mean? It means more than just saying, 'The book of Job contains knowledge (i. e. facts — the necessary information to make sense of something).' 'Wisdom', when applied to certain books of the Bible, identifies them as containing instruction on *how to live in this world to the glory of God*. In a sense, every book of the Bible contains such instruction; but some do so in very practical and 'down-to-earth' ways. The 'wisdom' books show us how to live as God intends us to live.

Being wise, in Bible terms, is set against the backdrop of our relationship to God. Unless we 'know God' (through faith in Jesus Christ alone) and walk in his ways, we are fools. As Jesus said: 'And everyone who hears these words of mine and does not do them will be like a foolish man who built his house on the sand' (Matt. 7:26).

Reverencing God is crucial. Depending upon him, walking humbly before him, worshipping him at every point of our lives is the way of wisdom. Wise people, the Bible insists, glorify God and enjoy him in all circumstances.

> Even in pain!
> Even when life turns bitter!
> Even when dreams are shattered!
> Even when nightmares become reality!
> Even when we secretly think that God is a 'cosmic sadist',
>   as C. S. Lewis once confessed.[1]

For your journal...

1. As you begin this study of Job, write down what your expectations are. What kind of questions do you think the book of Job is going to answer?

2. What is the significance of the opening verse of Job?

3. Since the book of Job is classified as part of the 'wisdom' literature of the Bible, what does this tell us about the overall purpose of the story?

Day 2
The soul of godliness

Job 1

'Now there was a day when the sons of God came to present themselves before the LORD, and Satan also came among them'
(Job 1:6).

Suggested reading: Job 1:1-8

Job is introduced to us as coming from Uz (1:1), which is thought to have been somewhere in the Arabian Desert. He is *not* an Israelite, but a representative of humanity at large. He has no recorded lineage, but his anonymity helps us identify with him.

The book of Job begins with a prologue of two chapters in length. It is important to realize that the prologue is written for *our* benefit! Job himself had not read it, and he was unaware of the universal drama that unfolds within it. For Job, the trial 'just came', from 'out of the blue', as we sometimes say euphemistically, without foreknowledge or inkling on his part.

To set the scene, we are going to be told something about Job that will make the point of the story all the more puzzling. Without this information, we might be tempted to think that Job was being punished for something.

And what is that we are told? Job was one of the godliest men of his time!

We all expect ungodly people to suffer even if that is, so often, not the case. When we fall into trouble, we say instinctively, 'What have I done to deserve this?' The rule of the universe is, we suspect, that good is rewarded and evil is punished. That belongs to the moral fabric of the universe. Otherwise the very heart of Christianity falls apart. Right?

The problem is that the world is not as we expect it to be. Bad people live lives of luxury and ease. Good people seem always to be troubled. It is the tension Asaph, the Jerusalem Temple Choir Director, struggled with as he relates in Psalm 73:

> For I was envious of the arrogant
>   when I saw the prosperity of the wicked…
> All in vain have I kept my heart clean
>   and washed my hands in innocence.
> For all the day long I have been stricken
>   and rebuked every morning
>
> (Ps. 73:3, 13-14).

This is exactly the conundrum established in the opening chapter of Job. It is not just that a righteous man is suffering; it is the trial of one of the godliest men in the world!

A twofold testimony as to the character of Job is given, one by the author (1:1), and another by God himself (1:8). To stress the latter: *God* tells us that Job was a godly man. We need to make a note of that. Whatever else may be going on here, God's assessment of Job is that he was godly. Whatever Job's comforters may say (and they will have a great deal to say), whatever Job himself may protest (and he will protest much, too much!), *and whatever we may secretly begin to imagine,* God himself testifies as to his piety.

Something extraordinarily important emerges straight away: the reason for his suffering must lie outside of any personal sin on Job's part. There exists a situation which we may call (and has been called) 'innocent suffering'.

But we run ahead of ourselves. Lest we miss the point, the prologue gives even more testimony to Job's godliness, using four words to describe it: he is *blameless, upright, reverent* and *consecrated.* If we substitute 'wholehearted' for 'blameless' we will get a better sense of it and avoid any suggestion of sinlessness on Job's part. Job is not going to be punished for his sin, but that does not mean that he is not a sinner!

What is said about Job here could easily describe how the Bible (Old *and* New Testaments) understands the nature of true godliness, and therefore the model of true piety. These four words could well describe the very essence of that 'holiness without which no one will see the Lord' (Heb. 12:14). There is a maturity to Job's piety that is due to its inherent God-centred focus. When Paul encapsulates the threefold goal of all God's work, namely, 'to the praise of the glory of his grace' (Eph. 1:6, 12, 14), he is saying theologically what the opening of the book of Job is saying biographically. 'For from him and through him and to him are all things. To him be glory for ever. Amen' (Rom. 11:36). Job finds his contentment in God, and this, as John Piper in our day is fond of saying, citing Jonathan Edwards of the eighteenth century, is how God is most glorified. Job is a role model here, make no mistake about it.

Job had a healthy respect for God. Not to fear God is a sickness of the soul. The fear of God is what godliness is all about. It is an apprehension of God in majesty held before our eyes. Job had a great God and he knew it! When we fear God, as a rendition of Psalm 34 by Isaac Watts puts it: 'we will have nothing else to fear'!

There is nothing better than to be subject to the majesty of God.

Job was godly and it showed. He was a man of spiritual and moral integrity, and bore the distinguishing marks of true religion. Like bookends, God calls Job, 'my servant...', signalling his love for him (1:8; 42:7-8). He is set up for us as a model husband and father, offering burnt offerings on behalf of his children and ensuring their purification according to the established rites. Job is concerned lest they may have 'cursed' God in their hearts (1:5; the Hebrew text says 'bless' here, as it does again in 2:9, but 'curse' is what is meant. The ancient writers thought it inappropriate to write 'curse' next to the divine name).

This makes Job's plea of 'innocence' plausible. His friends will accuse him of all kinds of sins and indiscretions; but we know that whatever the reason for Job's suffering, it is not *directly* connected to any sin he has committed. That is not to say that Job does not sin *during* the trial — he most assuredly does! He will have to confess in the end that he has spoken out of turn (40:4-5; 42:3). But for now at least, we are being introduced to a man of God whose assurance of God's grace to him lies in atonement and sacrifice, as the burnt offerings on behalf of his children indicates. Job rests in the assurance of his relationship with God secured by blood.

Later in the Old Testament, Job is mentioned alongside Daniel and Noah as widely-known men of God (Ezek. 14:14, 20). It is all the more shocking, then, that Job, of all people, should suffer in the way that he does.

Why is it that 'good' people suffer? This is the tension set up in these opening lines of the book.

This is faith *on trial.*

For your journal...

1. What does it mean for you to fear God? Are there areas of your life in which this fear is not displayed? Ask yourself the question: Would someone ever write about me, that I reverence God? Note some areas that may have to change for this observation to be more accurate.

2. Begin to think through the issue of 'innocent suffering'. What are some of the problems associated with this notion? We will have to return to this many times before we have finished our study of the book of Job!

3. Reflect on the words of Peter: 'Beloved, do not be surprised at the fiery trial when it comes upon you to test you, as though something strange were happening to you' (1 Peter 4:12). What are some of the ways in which we might demonstrate 'surprise'?

Day 3
'The prince of darkness'

Job 1

'Then Satan answered the LORD and said,
"Does Job fear God for no reason?
Have you not put a hedge around him
and his house and all that he has, on every side?
You have blessed the work of his hands,
and his possessions have increased in the land.
But stretch out your hand and touch all that he has,
and he will curse you to your face"'
(Job 1:9-11).

Suggested reading: Job 1:9-22

Behind every evil thing lies the menacing figure of Satan. The devil is, as they say, in the details.

We know this, but we are often prone to forget it. That is why the Bible keeps reminding us that from the beginning, when sin entered the world, along with pain and sickness, the devil was there. He had something to do with it.

It is still surprising, however, that Satan does not loom large in the Old Testament. Apart from here, in the opening chapters of Job, the only other chapters that mention his work in any detail are Genesis 3 and Zechariah 3.

Immediately, that should tell us something about how the Bible regards this prince of darkness. His powers are limited, so the Bible does not expend a great deal of time focusing on him. His powers are considerable and more malevolent than we can ever imagine; but they are no match for the powers of God. Remember how Martin Luther put it?

And though this world with devils filled,
Should threaten to undo us,
We will not fear, for God hath willed
His truth to triumph through us.
The prince of darkness grim,
We tremble not for him;
His rage we can endure,
For lo! His doom is sure;
One little word shall fell him.

The word 'Satan' means 'to bear a grudge (against), to oppose'. Here, it is used with the definite article, '*the* Satan'. It is a title as much as it is a name, and is descriptive of what he is. He is the 'adversary', that 'roaring lion, seeking someone to devour' (1 Peter 5:8). He is the 'father of lies' (John 8:44).

He is in this story because his every moment is consumed with hatred for God. Since Job is one of God's children, Satan seeks to prove that the only reason Job worships God is because, thus far at least, life has been good to him. Take that away and you will see Job deserting the ship of grace in an instant (see 1:9-11).

In effect, this story is about God's sovereignty over Satan as much as it is about God's work in the life of Job. There are greater questions behind this story than the one that immediately concerns Job — cosmic questions like:

- Who is in ultimate control?
- Can God deliver what he has promised?
- Is the grace of God invincible?

One of the first things that often puzzles those who read this story is the fact that Satan is *in the presence of God* (1:6; 2:1)! How can that be? Several truths emerge that will clarify what is being said here.

In response to the question 'Where is this taking place?' the best thing we can do is to plead ignorance. That may not be very satisfactory, but we know that this is not heaven. Satan cannot enter heaven. No sin nor evil can step across the threshold of that holy place. But Satan is *somewhere*. And what is far more important is the question, '*Why* is he there?'

Satan, along with the 'angels' (the Hebrew reads 'sons of God'), came to 'present themselves before the LORD' (1:6). Satan has to give an account of himself! Imagine how galling that must be! He does not have ultimate authority. He is 'reporting' to God. He is not autonomous; his power has been delegated to him. That should tell us immediately that his power is curtailed. He cannot do as he pleases. His malice is under check. It may not appear like that to us, but whatever wickedness he can design, it is always less than he might desire.

When Satan says that he has been 'wandering' about the earth, he betrays something about himself: he is a vagrant, a vagabond. He roams through the earth, going back and forth (1:7). He spends his time wandering to and fro. He can never say, 'This is my home.'

Philosophically, this tells us that ultimate reality is not dualistic. In other words, good and evil are not equally powerful in the universe. It may seem that way, but good outweighs evil in the ultimate view of things. Satan's power is not on a par with

God's. There is no equality between good and evil. As Calvin says in his *Institutes of the Christian Religion*: 'God holds the key.'[1]

Trials come as a result of Satan's malice. Job was unaware of that, of course. He never gives Satan a mention. That is one of Satan's tricks. He is quite content that we never give him a moment's thought, so that he can get on with his work without hindrance!

However, trials cannot simply be attributed to Satan. They *can* be attributed to him, but not *solely* to him. It is God who brings up the possibility of Job's temptation to Satan (1:8; 1:12; 2:3). This is so very important to understand. The ultimate authority for this trial is God's, not Satan's. When bad things happen to God's people, *God does it*! That is the disturbing message. We get the impression that Satan had not even thought about Job until God mentioned him.

Satan is a cynic! He always misreads and twists everything. 'Does Job fear God for no reason?' (1:9), he says. In effect, he suggests the only reason why Job does not curse God is because of the things God has given to him. Take these away and Job will curse God to his face. That gives us a clue as to Satan's ultimate purpose: to curse God. He will do it himself, and he will attempt to get others to join him. That is what he lives for. It is hard to imagine a being so utterly given over to evil as to make this the goal of everything.

Satan has to live with the frustration that he can never accomplish what he desires. He is limited in his abilities. He is not omnipotent; he is a finite creature. God sets boundaries around what he can and cannot do (1:11; cf. 2:6). Job can be tested domestically and circumstantially, but he himself (initially, at least) must remain unscathed. There are 'rules of engagement'. At the close of the Bible, we see it again in

Revelation 20, where Satan is 'released' for a season from his captivity; but only to fulfil God's plan.

Satan's defeat is certain.

You can make *too much* of the devil! He may be doing his worst, but he is not the ultimate source of power. Remember what Jesus said to Peter: 'Simon, Simon, behold, Satan demanded to have you, that he might sift you like wheat, but I have prayed for you that your faith may not fail' (Luke 22:31-32).

For your journal...

1. C. S. Lewis once remarked that we can make two equally bad errors with regard to Satan: we can make too much of him or we can make too little of him. Reflect on this as you read and study this opening chapter of Job.

2. Reflect on the words of Peter: 'Be sober-minded; be watchful. Your adversary the devil prowls around like a roaring lion, seeking someone to devour' (1 Peter 5:8); and/or those of John: 'Whoever makes a practice of sinning is of the devil, for the devil has been sinning from the beginning. The reason the Son of God appeared was to destroy the works of the devil' (1 John 3:8).

3. What are some of the points of tension in asserting on the one hand the sovereignty of God, and on the other the 'freedom' of Satan to do his evil work? Can you suggest some ways in which these points of tension can be relieved?

Day 4
The sovereignty of God

Job 1

*'And the LORD said to Satan, "Have you considered my servant Job,
that there is none like him on the earth, a blameless and upright man,
who fears God and turns away from evil?"' (Job 1:8).*

Suggested reading: Job 1:1-22

The disturbing thing in the story of Job is the realization that behind what happens to him lies the hand of God. There is no avoiding it. It is not so much that Job suffered. We are used to that happening, and see examples of it every day.

No, the problem here is God!

Stating it like that is shocking, isn't it? How can God be a 'problem'? But the issue we have to face is this: how can God *allow* this to happen?

Indeed, it is stronger than that. As Calvin observes in the opening chapters of the *Institutes of the Christian Religion*, it is not a matter of God 'allowing' this or that, as though he was somehow passive in all of this. God actually instigates the trial. He puts the idea in Satan's head. 'Have you considered my servant Job?' (1:8; cf. 2:3).

The suffering is God's doing. *That* is the problem.

The sovereignty of God extends over everything and everyone. Even the kingdom of darkness is subject to the rule of God. As theologians like to call it, the issue is one of *theodicy*. How can God's justice be maintained in the face of the suffering of a man like Job?

We may want to rush to the conclusion that 'there is none righteous, no not one'; that what Job experiences is what every sinner would endure apart from the grace of God. However, that would be to miss the point established by the testimony already given to Job's godliness. The point is that Job's suffering has nothing to do with his sin. How, then, can suffering be explained without, on the one hand, impugning the righteous character of God, or, on the other hand, calling into question God's sovereignty over Satan? In terms stated often in the past, either God is sovereign, in which case he is not good; or, God is good and he is not sovereign.

The latter possibility has been ruled out already. Satan cannot lift a finger without God's command: 'And the LORD said to Satan, "Behold, all that he has is in your hand. Only against him do not stretch out your hand." So Satan went out from the presence of the LORD... And the LORD said to Satan, "Behold, he is in your hand; only spare his life"' (1:12; 2:6).

So, what are we left with? The possibility that God is sovereign *but not good*?

Putting it like that reminds us again that the book of Job is primarily a book about God. It is the issue we shall have to return to again and again as we unfold its message. It is not so much a case of 'Why do we suffer?' but rather, 'Why does *God make us suffer?*' When we come full circle to the end of the book, we shall observe that Job is given a revelation of the majesty of God rather than an answer to his many questions.

Job loses everything. *Everything!*

To lose one child is a blow too horrible to describe. But to lose all ten children at once? Few of us, mercifully, can relate to it. This is not just suffering, it is a parent's worst nightmare. In one day, Job is rendered bankrupt and destitute. It is difficult to imagine anything more awful than this.

It tells us immediately that no Christian is exempt from such horrible possibilities. Coming to faith in Jesus Christ does not guarantee us a passport to a life of ease and luxury. It is all too possible to be a faithful servant of Christ and suffer horribly. Whatever contemporary Christianity may say, health and wealth is not a guarantee of godliness and Christian discipleship. Indeed, Jesus seems to warn us of the very opposite: 'If anyone would come after me, let him deny himself and take up his cross and follow me' (Matt. 16:24).

For now, Job's response is to 'worship' (1:20). It is the most sublime thing in the entire book. It is what we desire of ourselves if we were to find ourselves victims of a similar trial. But would we?

It is always appropriate to worship. We read of martyrs in the moments before their execution giving worship to God in the most exquisite ways.

Job seems utterly submissive and servant-like. The events do not seem to have unhinged him. It is the epitome of trust. The beautiful words of verse 21 are stunning:

Naked I came from my mother's womb,
And naked shall I return.
The LORD gave and the LORD has taken away;
Blessed be the name of the LORD

(1:21).

Several things emerge from these words. Job seems to be saying,

- this world is not my ultimate home;
- God's purpose transcends this life;
- everything that happens to us is from God;
- we must never attribute to God anything that is evil.

Yes, Job is acknowledging God's sovereignty over his life. In the immediate aftermath of his initial trial (another blow is coming in chapter 2), Job is not asking the major questions. His concern is to rest in the Lord's mercy and promise. If Job had questions, he did not utter them.

Nevertheless, here is a mystery:

- God foreordains everything that comes to pass;
- God is not the author of sin;
- God does not tempt us to sin;
- God does not condone sin.

How can this be? How can God ordain the occurrence of evil and remain free from the charge of being evil himself? This has been the problem of pain from the very beginning. Theologians have not always tried to answer it, partly because the answer involves grasping difficult concepts. And most answers are unsatisfying. The Westminster Divines of the seventeenth century were content merely to state the issue without any attempt to reconcile: 'God from all eternity, did, by the most wise and holy counsel of His own will, freely, and unchangeably ordain whatsoever comes to pass: yet so, as thereby neither is God the author of sin...'[1]

Sometimes all we can do is state what is true; logic evades us.

James Robertson's biography of Stonewall Jackson contains a beautiful and moving account of the time when, at thirty years of age, Jackson lost his wife Ellie, and baby son. On Sunday afternoon, 22 October 1854, Ellie went into labour. The child was stillborn. About an hour later Ellie began to haemorrhage and died very quickly. Writing to his sister Laura, Jackson stated:

> I have been called to pass through the deep waters of affliction, but all has been satisfied. The Lord giveth and the Lord taketh away, blessed be the name of the Lord. It is his will that my dear wife and child should no longer abide with me, and as it is His holy will, I am perfectly reconciled to the sad bereavement, though I deeply mourn my loss. My Dearest Ellie breathed her last on Sunday evening, the same day on which the child was born dead. Oh! The consolations of religion! I can willingly submit to anything if God strengthens me. Oh! My Sister, would that you could have Him for your God! Though all nature to me is eclipsed, yet I have joy in knowing that God withholds no good things from them that love and keep his commandments. And he will overrule this *Sad, Sad* bereavement for good.

A few weeks later he wrote again:

> She has now gone on a glorious visit through a gloomy portal. I look forward with delight to the day when I shall join *her*. Religion is all that I desire it to be. I am

reconciled to my loss and have joy in hope of a future reunion when the wicked cease from trembling and the weary are at rest.[2]

Job would have said the same. *Can you?*

For your journal...

1. Your own trials may appear trivial in comparison with Job's. Nevertheless, they remain trials with which you wrestle each day. If God is sovereign in these trials, as the Bible insists, reflect on the ways you have responded to them so far. Compare your response to that of Job.

2. We began the chapter by suggesting that the 'problem' has more to do with God himself than anything (or anyone) else. Why?

3. Reflect on the words of Jesus: 'If anyone would come after me, let him deny himself and take up his cross and follow me' (Matt. 16:24).

Day 5
It never rains but it pours

Job 2

'Again there was a day when the sons of God came to present themselves before the Lord, and Satan also came among them to present himself before the Lord' (Job 2:1).

Suggested reading: Job 2:1-10

Job has lost everything! His livelihood, his possessions, and all of his children — *all ten of them in one fell swoop!*

It is difficult to imagine a greater trial than that. Job's response has been breathtaking:

> Naked I came from my mother's womb,
> And naked shall I return.
> The Lord gave and the Lord has taken away;
> Blessed be the name of the Lord
>
> (1:21).

That was yesterday and today is another 'day' (2:1).

It never rains but it pours, we sometimes say. Chapter 2 opens with a chilling account of how Job suddenly becomes very ill. Satan is reporting on his movements and again, God brings up the case of Job! 'Have you considered my servant Job?' (2:3).

Indeed he had! But even Satan may have been taken aback at the knowledge that he is to be given a second chance to attack Job, seeing as though he had failed even to make so much as a dent in Job's armour the first time around. 'He still holds fast his integrity…' God says (2:3). Satan has been unsuccessful in getting Job to curse God! So far, at least, Satan has lost the wager.

Some trials will incite us to think evil of God; to think the unthinkable: that God does not know, does not understand, does not care! That is how Satan wants us to react in our pain: to think bad thoughts about God, that God may have acted against Job 'without reason' (2:3).

Some trials do seem purposeless. They are devoid of any reason, any explanation that might give them some validity. This thought is deeply troubling. After all, what keeps us going in dark times is the belief that somewhere, somehow, there lies a reason for the mess we find ourselves in. The idea that providence may lack purpose and direction is not comforting. The idea that even God himself is subject to arbitrariness is a chilling thought indeed.

Though God does say that Job's test had been 'without reason', he means this only as far as our perception of it might be. Satan obviously could see no sense in it, and neither could Job. But does that mean that there was no reason *at all*? That even God could not account for it? That somehow God had given in to irrationality and whim?

Of course not! As the book of Job will make clear, there is always a reason behind everything that happens. Providence is never arbitrary. God works all things together for the good of those that love him (Rom. 8:28). He works *all things* according to the counsel of his will (Eph. 1:11). There are no 'black holes' in God's governance of the universe. His control is absolute and purposeful. We may not understand the purpose, but that is not to say that it does not exist.

In one of my commentaries on Job I currently keep a letter from a friend, which reads this way:

> 'I have pretty much given up trying to read providence, but I wonder if you are in one of those *hinnam* [the Hebrew word used here], "without cause", "gratuitous" trials like your friend Job (2:3…).'

Some of life's troubles seem random and purposeless. They are not, of course, but they do appear that way. As Tennyson would say of the charge of the Light Brigade with all its tragic consequences:

> Theirs is not to reason why
> Theirs is but to do and die:
> Into the valley of Death
> Rode the six hundred.

In this light, Job's response is all the more remarkable. Especially when *another* trial comes, which renders him so ill that it seemed as though he would eventually die from it.

Satan is allowed to inflict Job with disease, but a boundary is established: he is to 'spare his life' (2:6).

Health is a sensitive issue, particularly for Christians in the West. A casual observer might be forgiven for suggesting that the modern church views health as a 'right' rather than a privilege. Many of our prayer meetings have become 'organ recitals' as one health issue after another becomes the focus of our praying, at the expense of other issues like evangelism and discipleship.

Sickness is sometimes thought to be *in itself* evidence of misshapen spirituality. We ought not to be sick! We forget that folk like Timothy, Trophimus, Epaphroditus, and even Paul, were sick!

Job's condition is all the more graphically portrayed when the writer describes him scraping off sores with bits of broken pottery as he sat on the city's refuse site (2:8). Later, Job's disease is described in even more detail. It includes such symptoms as aching, rotting bones (30:17), dark and peeling skin (30:28, 30), wart-like eruptions (7:5), anorexia (19:20), fever (30:30), depression (7:16; 30:15), insomnia (7:4), nightmares (7:14), putrid breath (19:17), failing vision (16:16), rotting teeth (19:20). Little wonder when Job's friends first meet him at the close of this chapter, 'they could hardly recognize him' (2:12)!

Sickness is something Christians can expect. We ought not to be surprised when we fall ill. After all — and it is a point which simplistic views of faith-healing ignore — we are all going to die one day of some sickness or other, unless Christ returns to prevent it.

It is Job's response that steals all the thunder: 'Shall we receive good from God, and shall we not receive evil?' (2:10).

Job's understanding of God includes the idea that he can send trouble. Job's view is not that when bad things happen, God has no part in it! What possible comfort would that be? What kind of God would that be? Right at the heart of the trouble is the beating heart of God!

What Job is saying is that not only good things, but also bad things can work together for our good. 'Before I was afflicted I went astray, but now I keep your word,' testified the psalmist (Ps. 119:67).

A quick word about Mrs Job! She too had experienced the same loss as her husband. She, too, experienced the pain of losing her ten children — unimaginable pain! And what Job has feared for his own children, she now openly encourages: 'Curse God and die,' she urged (2:9). What did she mean?

According to Augustine, she was *diaboli adjutrix* — the devil's advocate! According to Calvin she was *organum satani* — the tool of Satan! And Aquinas suggested that Satan had spared her in order to use her against her husband!

But perhaps some sympathy is in order! Is she really some 'second Eve' tempting her husband to sin? Is she so filled with anger and revenge that all she can now think of is causing God as much injury as possible?

Perhaps not. She may have seen that her husband is dying and she does not want him to suffer unduly, so she urges him to get it over with quickly by cursing God and suffering the consequences in some sort of instantaneous divine retribution. Whatever her exact intention, Job regarded her words as 'foolish', that is, as siding with unbelief rather than the way of faith.

Wisdom submits to the providence of God
rather than fights against it.

The story of Horatio Spafford is well known. Having experienced financial disaster in the fires of Chicago in 1873, he sent his wife and four children to England aboard the ship SS *Ville de Havre*. Halfway across the Atlantic, it collided with another ship, the SS *Lochearn*. Over 200 people were drowned, including Spafford's four children. Upon reaching the shores of England, Mrs Spafford sent a telegram, which read, 'Saved Alone'. Her husband caught the next boat across in order to be with her and, it is said, when the boat stopped at the point where the sinking had occurred, Spafford wrote these lines:

> When peace, like a river, attendeth my way,
> When sorrows like sea billows roll;
> Whatever my lot, Thou hast taught me to say,
> 'It is well, it is well with my soul.'

For your journal...

1. In the event of a possible future trial, outline some of the ways in which you would hope to respond to it. For example, what kind of things would you want to say as you try to deal with the situation? It is easier, of course, to think about this now than at the time when the trial comes. The Holy Spirit can give us words that would surprise us in situations of difficulty, but it may help us to outline what a biblical response to trials would look like.

2. Reflect on the words of Paul, 'In him we have obtained an inheritance, having been predestined according to the purpose of him who works all things according to the counsel of his will' (Eph. 1:11).

3. What are some of the consequences of the notion that God is not in control of the future, or, to use a current phrase, that the future is 'open' to God and not predetermined?

4. Reflect on the words of Peter, 'For what credit is it if, when you sin and are beaten for it, you endure? But if when you do good and suffer for it you endure, this is a gracious thing in the sight of God. For to this you have been called, because Christ also suffered for you, leaving you an ex-ample, so that you might follow in his steps' (1 Peter 2:20-21).

Day 6
Gloom and deep darkness

Job 3

'Let the day perish on which I was born,
    and the night that said,
      "A man is conceived."
Let that day be darkness!
May God above not seek it,
    nor light shine upon it.
Let gloom and deep darkness claim it.
Let clouds dwell upon it;
let the blackness of the day terrify it'
      (Job 3:3-5).

Suggested reading: Job 3:1-7

For seven days Job has grieved in silence. Three friends, Eliphaz, Bildad and Zophar, have joined him, but have so far said nothing (2:13). There are times when words fail. There are times when silence is the best therapy.

But then comes chapter 3! Here are waters too deep for some to fathom. 'After this Job opened his mouth and cursed the day of his birth' (3:1).

Shocking, isn't it? We will look at Job's experience in greater detail in the next chapter, but it will help us understand something of great significance if we pause and reflect on this in general here.

Can Christians ever say things like this? Can a Christian ever wish he had never been born? Do we explain away Job's response as somehow belonging to the Old Testament, when, as is sometimes supposed, believers found themselves saying things because they did not have the full revelation enjoyed by New Testament saints? To suggest such a thing betrays a naivety about Christian experience that is breathtaking!

Gerard Manley Hopkins wrote a poem, in which he said,

O the mind, mind has mountains; cliffs of fall
Frightful, sheer, no-man-fathomed. Hold them cheap
   May who ne'er hung there.

Let's ask again: does our understanding of what a Christian is include such feelings as these? Before we answer, we need to recall that Jeremiah used almost identical language to depict his own experience in Jeremiah 20:14-18. And some of the psalms, especially Psalms 57 and 88, paint as gloomy a picture as we have here. As Hopkins suggests, those 'who ne'er hung there' may well judge Job harshly. They may find it difficult to believe that Christians can speak like this.

Job is giving vent to how he feels and before we rush in and condemn, we need to listen to him. We need to ask ourselves whether we have ever felt like this? And we should especially note the *patience* of God as he responds to Job's outburst — with silence!

The point is that Job is not alone in these dark moods. We have already mentioned Jeremiah and the psalmist. The case of Elijah, sitting beneath a juniper tree, wishing that his life be taken away, is also well known (1 Kings 19), although it seems to me that the text of 1 Kings 19 may suggest that Elijah is not so much depressed as fatalistic. He is not quite the psychological wreck that so many commentators make him out to be! His desire for death seems to spring from his view that one way or another he is going to die and he would prefer that it was not by the hands of Jezebel's forces, lest she be seen to triumph over the kingdom of God.

Calvin once wrote that the Psalms contained 'an anatomy of all the parts of the soul'. The human soul is capable of a variety of moods and responses, including the dark and sombre tones of this chapter. Denial of this will lead to a distorted view of humanity; but, more importantly, it will lead to a distorted view of the gospel which ministers to such responses.

That seems to be the point of this third chapter of Job. We are given a glimpse of a soul in distress not least to ensure that we do not draw the wrong conclusions when we are tempted to experience similar days of darkness.

Something far more poignant needs to shine into this darkness. It is the response of Jesus in Gethsemane, where Jesus is described as 'greatly distressed and troubled' (Mark 14:33; cf. Matt. 26:37).

There is a sinful way to express these emotions, but they are not in themselves *necessarily* sinful. Jesus experiences something in Gethsemane that causes his soul to recoil, and he utters a desire that 'this cup pass' from him. 'And going a little farther he fell on his face and prayed, saying, "My Father, if it be possible, let this cup pass from me; nevertheless, not as I will, but as you will"' (Matt. 26:39). 'And he said to them, "My soul is very sorrowful, even to death. Remain here and watch"' (Mark 14:34).

Jesus expressed the longing that providence might unfold in a different way than it apparently does. At no point does he express rebellion. Nor does he ever fail to yield obedience to God's will; but that does not exclude the possibility that he may long for providence to be different, *and to do so without at any point committing sin.* Jesus walked through darker valleys in Gethsemane than we can ever imagine, and he uttered the longing that he could accomplish God's purposes in some other way.

What this says is crucially important. It is not that Job is devoid of sin in what he says in this chapter; not at all! But before we rush in to condemn, we must allow for the possibility that the darkest thoughts can be expressed in a way that is without sin. Failure to do so impugns the impeccability of our Saviour.

Some experiences can only be responded to in the minor key. To suggest otherwise, as some saccharin-saturated expressions of Christianity do, is to rob countless numbers of God's people of hope when they need it most. That is why formulaic expressions of a true life of discipleship, like the one popularized in the Prayer of Jabez, for example, are not only deficient, but also harmful.

We cannot counsel in something we do not really appreciate. If we cannot understand why some Christians 'sing the blues', we will not be in a position to help them. This, in many ways, was the error of Job's friends, as we shall see. It is precisely for this reason that Jesus is portrayed for us in the Gospels as one 'made like his brothers in every respect' (Heb. 2:17). He was 'greatly distressed and troubled ... very sorrowful even to death' (Mark 14:33-34).

He understands the complexities of the human psyche to a degree that is altogether sublime.

Spiritual maturity doesn't always live on the mountain top!

There is a popular view of Christianity that suggests that unless you are experiencing miracles every day, then somehow you are not living to your full potential. That is untrue! That would call into question great tracts of Jesus' life and ministry.

When life turns sour, spiritual maturity shows itself in our ability at such times to go into the closet and pour out our woes to God. When Jesus was in Gethsemane was he displaying spiritual maturity? It is a question we do not even need to ask, isn't it? But if Jesus could be without sin, yet remain mature in the darkness of those moments, there are times in our darkness when to utter a cry would display the same maturity.

Perhaps that is what you need to do right now: pour out your woes to him who sees every tear (Ps. 56:8).

For your journal...

1. In Psalm 88, the psalmist says:

   'You have put me in the depths of the pit,
       in the regions dark and deep.
   Your wrath lies heavy upon me,
       and you overwhelm me with all your waves'

   (Ps. 88:6-7).

   Perhaps like Job, and the psalmist here, you can relate all too easily to these sentiments. What can we learn from their inclusion within the Bible?

2. Are there any limitations to the degree of depression a Christian can experience?

3. Reflect on the words of Jesus: 'My soul is very sorrowful, even to death' (Mark 14:34).

Day 7
Singing the blues

Job 3

'Why did I not die at birth,
come out from the womb and expire?'
(Job 3:11).

Suggested reading: Job 3:8-26

The sudden change of tone from the end of chapter 2 to the beginning of chapter 3 is so intense that some explanation seems necessary. What had happened that could explain this? Several things.

First, time has passed by. A week (2:13) has transpired since Job's astonishing confession to his wife of his complete trust in the Lord's providence.

Time can often change our perspective on things. Many Christians have found themselves *upheld* at the moment of crisis, proving God's power in their lives. At such times they have responded with a sweetness that may even have surprised themselves, only to find that as days and weeks pass by, things change. Questions that never surfaced at the time now bubble up from somewhere within — dark questions, terrifying questions, accusatory questions.

Second, Job's friends have arrived. We shall have more to say about them later, but chapter 2 has introduced them to

us as those who desired to show 'sympathy' and 'comfort'
(2:11).

They have said nothing so far, in contrast to what is to
come. Surely, this is how it should be! We should empathize
before attempting to say anything. There is a time to be silent
(Eccles. 3:7).

By weeping, tearing their clothes, and sprinkling dust on
their heads, they had conveyed a sign that Job was dying (2:12).
Their demeanour signalled an imminent funeral. They were
mourning, not so much for Job's children as for Job himself.
Their body language indicated a hopelessness about Job. And
Job had begun to believe it.

Third, perhaps his wife had been right after all. Perhaps he
should curse God and die; get it over with as soon as possible.
Perhaps he should end this misery now, and call on God to
take him away. For seven days and nights he had pondered
the unthinkable. Unable to sleep, his body had begun to pound
with pain. With sorrow engulfing him, his physical weakness
made the temptation to despair all the more inviting.

Fourth, God had said nothing! He had been silent. And it
is the silence that often screams at us more loudly than anything else. The silence from 'outside' has caused Job to inter-
nalize his grief. Subliminally, he gives vent to cynicism, to a
spirit of nihilism, to despair, resentment and regret that bor-
ders on guilt. In the grieving process, Job has moved on from
confident trust to a nagging fear that he may have been duped.
'Where is God?' cried C. S. Lewis a month after his wife had
died, as he recorded his soul's journey through the dark chasm
of loss.

And Job is feeling this, too. He curses the day of his birth
(3:1). He wishes that that day would be removed from the
calendar (3:6); that the great sea-monster, Leviathan, would

swallow it up (v. 8); that the night in which the midwife said, 'It's a boy', may never have happened (v. 3). He wishes that the joy of that night be taken away (v. 7). He calls upon sooth-sayers, whose job it was to pronounce curses, to do just that upon the day which has brought nothing but trouble (vv. 8-9).

Every chapter in Job mentions death in some way. Here, Job depicts it in familiar terms as a 'shadow' (3:5, NIV). Psalm 23 uses the same expression, speaking of 'the shadow' it casts on the valley through which we sometimes walk (v. 4). 'I wish I'd never been born!' he says.

Job's life tastes 'bitter'; it has become a 'misery' (3:20). His life is full of 'sighing' and 'groanings' (v. 24). His worst night-mare has become a reality (v. 25). 'I have no peace, no quiet-ness; I have no rest, but only turmoil' (v. 26).

In verses 21-22, he depicts his desire for death with the same anticipation that a grave robber might have had. Grave robbery was a lucrative business, particularly in ancient Egypt when the dead were buried with many valuable possessions. They 'rejoice when they come to the grave' (v. 22), he says.

'Why do you keep wretched people like me alive?' Job asks in effect.

Are you shocked by this question? There are many more such questions in Job that we will uncover.

- Do you think I am made of stone or metal? (6:12)
- If life is short, does it also have to be miserable? (7:1-10)
- What did I ever do to become the target of your arrows? (7:20)
- You are the one who created me, so why are you destroying me? (10:8)
- Why do you hide your face and consider me your enemy? (13:24)

God allows us to ask questions like these! They may be mistaken. They may be the wrong questions. They may even come from faulty motivations. But we are allowed to ask them. And for now at least, God is going to be silent. There will come a time for rebuke, but not yet.

Joni Earecksen Tada has written:

'…make no mistake, Job's questions to God weren't of the polite Sunday school variety. They were pointed, sharp and seemed at times on the border of blasphemy… Tough, searching questions. Job's friends were horrified… And that, to me, is the comfort of the book of Job. What meant the most to me in my suffering was that God never condemns Job for his doubt and despair. God was even ready to take on the hard questions. Ah, but the answers? They weren't quite the ones Job was expecting.'[1]

Doubts! We should not have them, but we do. In his poem 'In Memoriam', written when a young friend was killed, Tennyson put it this way:

Perplexed in faith, but pure in deeds,
At last he beat his music out.
There lives more faith in honest doubt,
Believe me, than in half the creeds.

The point is that God knows how weak we are. He understands our frustrations and problems. Even when we step over the boundary, there are times when discipline must wait. God is patient with Job. He understands Job's fragility, his vulnerability.

Spiritual depression, to use an inexact term,
is a very real phenomenon.

'Why are you downcast, O my soul?
Why so disturbed within me?'

(Ps. 42:11, NIV).

'My soul is full of trouble
   and my life draws near the grave...
You have taken my companions and loved ones from me;
   the darkness is my closest friend'

(Ps. 88:3, 18, NIV).

The point of these passages in Scripture may well baffle us, but if we have no place for them in our understanding of the Christian life, we are seriously deficient. As we have seen before, if we cannot understand why some Christians 'sing the blues', we will not be in a position to help them. This is the constant failing of Job's friends.

On the other hand, Jesus understands us because he has been where we have been. As B. B. Warfield comments:

In these supreme moments our Lord sounded the ultim-ate depths of human anguish, and vindicated on the score of the intensity of his mental sufferings the right to the title Man of Sorrows. The scope of these sufferings was also very broad, embracing that whole series of painful emotions which runs from a consternation that is appalled dismay, through a despondency which is almost despair, to a sense of well-nigh desolation.[2]

Jesus, too, was a Man of Sorrows! There is a comfort to be drawn here that goes beyond words!

For your journal...

1. Outline some of the immediate reactions you may be having to Job's words in this chapter. Do you find yourself critical or sympathetic? Or both?

2. What would be the first words you would speak to Job after hearing this outburst?

3. Spend a few moments thinking of what your Saviour experienced in Gethsemane on your behalf. Write down the range of emotions he might have gone through. How does this help us to understand Job's response here? What does it teach you about something you (or a friend, or family member) may be passing through at the moment?

Day 8
The failure of counselling

Job 4 - 5

'Remember: who that was innocent ever perished?
Or where were the upright cut off?
As I have seen, those who plough iniquity
and sow trouble reap the same'
(Job 4:7-8).

Suggested reading: Job 4:1-11

'Remember: who that was innocent ever perished? Or where were the upright cut off?' (4:7).

Enter Job's friends!

They have sat in silence with Job as he grieved the loss of his children, and watched his body respond to some disease that threatens to take his life. As we have seen, sometimes it is right to say nothing.

But now the situation changes. Job's friends are no longer silent. They have something urgent to say to him and cannot contain it any more.

What is it that they say? There are some subtle nuances in the various contributions of Eliphaz, Bildad and Zophar. Eliphaz is probably the oldest and therefore speaks first. He is the philosopher of the three. His words carry a sense of importance — at least, they do to Eliphaz! Bildad is a traditionalist and comes across as, well, a little boring. Zophar is the young and somewhat arrogant bully. He does not mind what he says, even if he hurts in the process. He is determined to be heard.

Though these nuances exist, their message is essentially the same: 'They have no more songs but one, and have no regard at all to whom they sing it,' Calvin comments.[1] They are like a broken record, stuck in a groove, and repeating itself endlessly.

There is a wonderfully amusing Peanuts cartoon. Lucy, in that priggish manner of hers, says to Charlie Brown, 'There is one thing you are going to have to learn: you reap what you sow, you get out of life what you put in to it, no more and no less.' In the corner of the cartoon, Snoopy the dog is muttering, 'I'd kind of like to see a little margin for error.'

Job's friends think they know exactly what the problem is. Eliphaz even claims divine revelation for it (4:15-16). It is all very simple and straightforward:

'Remember: who that was innocent ever perished?
    Or where were the upright cut off?
As I have seen, those who plough iniquity
    and sow trouble reap the same'

(4:7-8).

There! Job has reaped what he has sown. He has brought this trouble on himself. He is responsible for the situation he now finds himself in. It is one of life's most basic principles. We are to blame for the troubles we get into.

It sounds correct, doesn't it? Christians, especially, are drawn into its simple, clean logic. In our 'post-modern' world, where everything is relative, such sureness is to be welcomed. Sin is punished, and it seems to make biblical sense to reverse the logic and suggest that what looks like punishment (suffering) must have, as its cause, the presence of sin.

This is a view that is widely believed in the church today. Christians who follow Jesus Christ with all of their hearts should not find themselves in trouble. God does not want his children to be sick. 'He wants the best for you,' we are told. We need to believe it. And it is our unbelief that accounts for the reason we find ourselves floundering. The 'health and wealth gospel', or 'prosperity gospel' — call it what you will — makes this very thing their central theme: God does not want his children to be in trouble. Christians must 'name it and claim it', or 'gab and grab it' as some put it euphemistically.

And that is exactly what Eliphaz is saying here. Job may well be a godly man, but he has only himself to blame for his predicament. His fault may be minor (at least, in comparison to what Bildad will say later); but, fault there is, make no mistake about it.

It is all very subtle — at least, this time around it is. Eliphaz says things that sound true. And they are true — up to a point! For example:

'Can a mortal be more righteous than God?
    Can a man be more pure than his Maker?'
(4:17, NIV).

Job has never claimed to be more righteous than God, but that does not prevent Eliphaz from pressing his point. He may not have said that in so many words, but in effect, Job is claiming just what Eliphaz is saying. Job's claim to 'blamelessness' — a word which Eliphaz has used already (4:6) and perhaps had heard used a great deal about Job (cf. 1:1, 8; 2:3) — is suspect. There may be something *wanting* in Job after all.

Later in the discourse, Eliphaz adds to his accusations by saying,

> 'For affliction does not come from the dust,
>   nor does trouble sprout from the ground,
> but man is born to trouble
>   as the sparks fly upwards'
>
> (5:6-7).

Do you see what he is saying? Trouble does not just happen! There is always a reason for it. And, for Eliphaz, that reason has to have something to do with Job. Something is amiss in Job's life.

You can almost sense Eliphaz's certainty about his position now. Job is behaving badly.

> 'Blessed is the one whom God reproves;
>   therefore despise not the discipline of the Almighty'
>
> (5:17).

Correction! That's what lies behind Job's predicament. God is correcting him. And any fool knows that correction implies error, transgression, *sin*!

And speaking of *fools*, Eliphaz adds:

> 'Resentment kills a fool,
>   and envy slays the simple.
> I myself have seen a fool taking root,

but suddenly his house was cursed.
His children are far from safety,
    crushed in court without a defender'

(5:2-4, NIV).

Biting words! The reference to children being 'crushed' would have reminded Job particularly of his own dear ones, now dead, and the words would have wounded somewhere deep within. Perhaps it is not Job's wife who has been foolish (2:10), but Job himself.

Tomorrow we will examine this view of Eliphaz in some detail, but for now, let's pause and reflect on how Job might have taken this. I well remember visiting a friend dying of cancer. She was twenty-four hours away from death. She knew it and I knew it — not the exact amount of time left to her, but we both knew it was not going to be long. Her emaciated body was failing and death was written all over her. And she was at peace about it. At least she *was* at peace; that is, until a well-intentioned minister called between my visits and said: 'If only you had faith, God would heal you.' She was dying, my friend concluded in those dark moments, leaving her three teenage children and husband behind, *because of her lack of faith. And lack of faith is sin. It was all her fault.*

It is impossible to relate, now, how difficult it was to pull her back from her despair, to pour some hope into those dying moments. This minister's intentions had been honourable, I am sure, but his words had come from the lowest regions of hell. It was the voice of Satan and not of God.

Do not be surprised when evil appears dressed in white garments!
This is not cynicism, but an antidote to spiritual depression.

This dear woman was being asked to die *for God's glory*! The help she needed was in coming to terms with it and even, difficult as it was, to rejoice in it. Yes, rejoice — because knowing that this was God's will was the most liberating thing of all. I was able to assure her of the presence of Jesus in her final hours as she gasped for the breath of life that would not come. As she walked in the valley of shadow, the long arms of her Saviour reached down and held her, bringing her to himself. I believe with all of my heart that, in the end, she knew it to be so.

And the same is true for every child of God.

For your journal...

1. What do you make of Eliphaz's claim to divine revelation as the source of his contribution? Are there circumstances where you have made similar claims?

2. How is Eliphaz's theology similar to the modern 'prosperity gospel' theology?

3. Reflect on the words of Paul: 'Do not be deceived: God is not mocked, for whatever one sows, that will he also reap. For the one who sows to his own flesh will from the flesh reap corruption, but the one who sows to the Spirit will from the Spirit reap eternal life' (Gal. 6:7-8). What bearing, if any, do these words have on the theology of Eliphaz?

Day 9
Partial truths

Job 6 - 7

'I loathe my life; I would not live for ever.
Leave me alone, for my days are a breath'
(Job 7:16).

Suggested reading: Job 7:1-11

Yesterday, we began to look at the argument presented by Eliphaz in his first speech to Job. We noted that, in essence, he was alleging that the reason for Job's suffering lies in something he has done. Suffering is God's punishment for our sins.

What are we to make of this argument? Can we dismiss it out of hand? We have a suspicion that it is wrong, but our evangelical theology tugs at us, asking if this is perhaps the truth. After all, those of us who take the Bible seriously know that God does indeed punish sin, and that there is no one, *no one*, who is without sin (apart from our Saviour). Is Eliphaz correct in his assessment of Job's predicament?

Yes he is! Eliphaz is *partly* right! What he says is *partly* true. His theological analysis has merit, painful as it is to admit. God does punish wickedness and transgression. It is a consequence of his holiness. For the universe to remain moral, sin can never go unpunished.

At the end of the ages, the universe will experience God's retribution. 'But by the same word the heavens and earth that now exist are stored up for fire, being kept until the day of judgement and destruction of the ungodly' (2 Peter 3:7).

Sometimes, however, the punishment comes in this life rather than at the end of the ages. Consider the account in 2 Samuel 6, where Uzzah is 'struck down' (v. 7) for stabilizing the ark, just as it is about to topple over and fall to the ground. And if we are tempted to think that this is something that God only does in the Old Testament, there is the New Testament account of Ananias and Sapphira, both of whom die — over the price of a piece of property (Acts 5:1-11)!

Instant retribution is a very disturbing fact. We cannot dismiss Eliphaz's words too quickly, particularly if the reason for doing so is that we somehow think that such judgements of God are unfair, or inconsistent with the way we have come to think of God. A consistently *biblical* representation of God must keep in mind the fact that 'it is a fearful thing to fall into the hands of the living God' (Heb. 10:31).

But although what Eliphaz says is partly right, it is also partly wrong. Eliphaz has employed a truth without distinction. He has failed to discern all of the facts. His theology is watertight, rigid and principled; but it is also misapplied and inept. It has failed to discern exceptions.

For example, Eliphaz had no room in his system for the account recorded in John 9 of the boy that was born blind. In answer to the query from the disciples as to who had sinned, the man or his parents, Jesus said it was neither. The reason for his suffering lay in another direction altogether. It had nothing to do with the man's past, but everything to do with his future. His suffering, Jesus is saying, is not due directly to his sin. The boy was not *being punished for something that he, or his parents, had done.* He had been born blind in order that the works of God might be made manifest in him and, as a result, would have an effect upon generations of people who would thereafter read the story and profit from it. He suffered, not for any sin of his own, or any inherited guilt resulting from the sin of another, but in order to bring a blessing to others.

As a counsellor, Eliphaz is clumsy. He has jumped to conclusions without knowing the facts. Or, perhaps he did know them and chose to ignore them because his system of theology was so rigid that nothing could change it.

He has rushed in where angels fear to tread.

What was Job's response? Anger! Eliphaz is nothing but a bag of wind (6:26). His contribution was about as insipid as 'the white of an egg' (6:6, NIV). His words are a disappointment (6:20).

Anger! Yes, with his 'friends'. But, anger with God, too. 'I loathe my life; I would not live for ever. Leave me alone, for my days are a breath' (7:16). Pain has evacuated any sense of purpose to his existence. Nihilism has gained a foothold. There is no point to his life anymore.

In what sounds almost like a parody of Psalm 8, Job felt the loss of his *dignity.* His condition is worse than a slave. Sleeplessness has added to his agitation. He feels victimized. His body is racked with pain. His open, dirty sores are a constant reminder of the frailty of his life.

'Why me?' Job says (cf. 7:20). And we can understand why he asks it.

Towards the end of Job's reply, he says something quite extraordinary. Like a child who is angry with his parents and storms out, Job seems to say, 'You'll be sorry when I'm gone!'

'Why do you not pardon my transgression
    and take away my iniquity?
 For now I shall lie in the earth;
    you will seek me, but I shall not be'

(7:21).

Even in his pain, Job is still talking to his God. His words may be angry. He may be saying things now that are very different from those sanguine expressions in the opening chapters, but he has not lost his faith in God, even though he thinks God is being unfair.

Job has begun to believe Eliphaz's accusations. Maybe, after all, sin is the problem and forgiveness the resolution.

The devil is attacking Job, filling his mind with doubt. But Job knows nothing of that. He can only think it is God's doing. And he wants to know one thing: 'Why?'

We can understand that question all too well. We, too, have our questions that begin with 'Why…?'

Why not begin to write some of them down in your journal? You may not get an answer to them all. Perhaps none of them will be answered in the way you desire. Neither this book you are reading, nor the book of Job, nor the Bible, nor all the wisdom of this world may be sufficient to uncover the dark questions that haunt your soul. And, in part, that is the lesson Job will teach you: that sometimes you will have to trust in God even when he does not answer your questions.

Can you do that?

For your journal...

1. In what way is Eliphaz partly right when he asserts that we get what we deserve? Can you think of instances in your life when this has been true?

2. In what way does the knowledge of Satan's involvement in this trial change the way you understand the situation? Would it change your evaluation of your present circumstances to know that Satan was involved in them in some way?

3. Following on from the previous question, reflect on the words of Jesus, 'Simon, Simon, behold, Satan demanded to have you, that he might sift you like wheat,' (Luke 22:31).

Day 10
Looking for an arbitrator

Job 8 – 10

*'If I summoned him and he answered me,
I would not believe that he was listening to my voice'*
(Job 9:16).

Suggested reading: Job 9:1-16

Who will stand up for Job against these counsellors? This is how Eugene Peterson describes Job's anguish in Job 9:33-35:

> How I wish we had an arbitrator
>   to step in and let me get on with life —
> To break God's grip on me,
>   to free me from this terror so I could breathe again.
> Then I'd speak up and state my case boldly.
> As things stand, there is no way I can do it.[1]

We can almost feel Job's loneliness. His friends are proving to be of no help to him; in fact, they are accusing him of sin and pleading for repentance. But things are even worse than that: God is proving to be hostile. Job can find no way into his presence. He is cut off, alone, unable to make a case for himself. There is no one to sympathize; no one seems to care. Job is all alone in his grief and pain. Even if he could state his case, and God were to respond, Job says, 'I would not believe that he was listening to my voice' (9:16).

Satan may not have managed to get Job to curse God as he had suggested (1:11; 2:5), but he has managed to deceive him. He has made God out to be a tyrant: uncaring, unmoved, heartless, callous.

There is nothing in the world quite like the feeling of being all alone, without a comforter to help, or to understand. Ask the inmate in a prison cell; or the divorcee eating dinner in an apartment; or the widow who has just buried a loved one; or the single person who goes to bed and rises *alone*; or the misunderstood teenager whose weird clothes and body-piercing are a cry for attention in the loneliness of their existence. Job knows how they feel!

But there is another side to Job here — an argumentative, disputatious side. Words like 'dispute' (9:3, 14, NIV), 'argue' (9:14, NIV) and 'appeal' (9:15) reveal a side of Job that we haven't seen before. Gone, now, is the depressed, mournful response of chapter 3. Grief has turned into anger, melancholy into resentment. God seems distant and unapproachable; Job's cries go unheard. Job is not yet willing to suggest that God is unjust; but there is no justice to which Job can have recourse. And he will not lie down and play dead! Pushed into a corner by his friends' counsel, he lashes out like a wounded animal, biting and snarling because his own survival is at stake. His words are defensive; since no one else will speak for him, Job has to make his own case.

It is Bildad who has provoked him to this response. Bildad is less circumspect than Eliphaz had been. 'The words of your mouth,' Bildad had said, are 'a great wind' (8:2). They had signalled his confrontational manner.

But what had Bildad said that had annoyed Job so much? Bildad had asked one of those 'Have-you-stopped-beating-your-wife?' sorts of questions! Either way, Job was guilty no matter how he answered.

> 'Does God pervert justice?
> Does the Almighty pervert the right?'
>
> (8:3).

Of course God doesn't pervert justice! What could possibly be wrong with what Bildad has said? *Everything!*

Bildad's point is that Job is suffering because God's justice has *not* been perverted. The implication is clear enough: Job is suffering because God has inflicted him with just punishment. To suggest otherwise is to impugn God's integrity.

It never occurs to Bildad that there is any other explanation to Job's predicament. Suffering is always the result of God's punitive displeasure.

The sting in Bildad's words has been the use of the conjunction, 'if': '*if* you are pure and upright...' (8:6). Bildad isn't at all sure of Job's innocence, but he is conceding the point that his sin may be less severe than that of his children. They, after all, had died! That, he assures Job, was God giving them over 'into the hand of their transgression' (8:4). (Actually, there is no evidence at all that they had died as a judgement of God. True, Job was concerned about them, acting as priest and offering sacrifices on their behalf [1:5]; but the text does not disapprove of these family gatherings, which were perhaps birthday celebrations.)

Everything is very simple for Bildad: life can always be explained in terms of merit and reward. Sin is always punished and it is therefore possible to infer from suffering that some unrighteous act was its cause. Suffering is invariably an indication of transgression.

Bildad backs up his homespun philosophy with two equally commonplace illustrations. The first is that of a papyrus plant that dries up for lack of water (8:11-13). 'Such are the paths of all who forget God,' he adds (8:13). The second illustration is that of a spider's web (8:14-19), something frail and impermanent — like Job's confidence in his own argument of innocence. 'Behold, God will not reject a blameless man, nor take the hand of evildoers' (8:20). Like Eliphaz before him, Bildad, too, suspects that all these claims regarding Job's blamelessness are deeply suspect — even though Job will insist on it again (9:21; c.f. 4:6; 1:1, 8; 2:3). Bildad is sowing seeds of doubt as to Job's integrity and character. Job *must* be guilty.

This is 'cash-register' justice!

You get what you deserve, no more and no less.

There are no exceptions, no extenuating circumstances. None!

There is something hopelessly dark about this theology. And those who are subjected to it are often least able to cope with it. Their pain has already rendered them susceptible to the accusations of blame. Hopelessness feeds upon itself; despair finds refuge in guilt. And Job can only assert his innocence at the expense of sounding insufferably self-righteous. It is a 'lose-lose' situation.

It is into such circumstances as these that Jesus enters. Job can only cry for an 'arbitrator'. Job wants a lawyer?

Lawyers! We make jokes about them. We suspect their motives when defending clients we suspect are guilty! But if we find ourselves in trouble, a lawyer is just what we need!

And we *are* in trouble! We find ourselves the victims of 'outrageous fortune'. Things happen to us that make no sense. Our ability to defend ourselves against such forces is pitifully weak. Where can we find someone who will speak for us, who will take our case and plead it before the only throne that matters?

Jesus! For every child of God, he does just that! 'For because he himself has suffered when tempted, he is able to help those who are being tempted' (Heb. 2:18).

For your journal...

1. Think through the issue of Job's claim to innocence again. Are there any doubts beginning to emerge in your mind as you listen to Job's response to Bildad? Are you beginning to lose faith in Job's integrity? (If so, you need to go back and read the opening two chapters again!)

2. Job 9:33 is the first of several passages in the book that seem to warrant a Messianic interpretation. Think of how Jesus is the 'answer' to Job's trouble. How is Jesus the answer to *your* trouble?

3. In what ways does our study in Job so far produce a distrust of 'packaged' theology? In responding to this question, evaluate how your own theological system (and we all have one!) copes with issues like pain and suffering. [Only reformed theology, in my opinion, is strong enough to handle the book of Job! Do you agree?]

Day 11
In the dark

Job 8 - 10

'I shall be condemned;
why then do I labour in vain'
(Job 9:29).

Suggested reading: Job 9:16-35

'I loathe my life,' Job cries (10:1). He wishes God would leave him alone and let him die.

Eugene Peterson's rendition of it goes like this:

Isn't it time to call it quits on my life?
    Can't you let up, and let me smile just once
Before I die and am buried,
    before I'm nailed into my coffin, sealed in the ground,
And banished for good to the land of the dead,
    Blind in the final dark?[1]

Job is not going to get any justice from these friends of his:

'If I wash myself with snow
    and cleanse my hands with lye,
yet you will plunge me into a pit,
    and my own clothes will abhor me'

(9:30-31).

When bad things happen… When bad things happen, *who*, or *what*, is the cause of them? Job would not have any other answer but that it is God who is behind all things. He had said to his wife much the same thing in chapter 2: 'Shall we receive good from God, and shall we not receive evil?' (v. 10).

Like Job, Florence Nightingale once wrote in her diary for May 1851: 'My life is more difficult than almost any other kind… Is this not God?' If God really is sovereign, in one way or another, he is behind everything that happens, including evil things. That is the great dilemma. *That* is the problem of pain. And it has led Job into a dungeon of deep despair.

Every now and then, Job tries to reason his way out of the darkness. Chapter 9 contains one such attempt, where he resorts to the world of the courtroom.

If only he could appeal to God…

But supposing Job could summon God into the courtroom. Just suppose that Job could make God give an account of his actions — what then? 'How can a mortal be righteous before God?' he asks (9:2, NIV). Do not misunderstand this question. Job is not asking about justification in the sense that Paul does in Galatians or Romans. No! Job's point is not so much, 'How can I, a sinner, be made right with God who is altogether holy?' but, 'How can I, a righteous, but finite individual, be assured of justice before a God whose ways I can never fathom?'

'If one wished to contend with him,
  one could not answer him once in a thousand times'
                                                    (9:3).

Job's point is that God cannot really account for himself. To *whom* would he do that? 'Who will say to him, "What are you doing?"' (9:12). Nor can he be brought under our control ('God will not turn back his anger...', 9:13). He is incomprehensible (he 'does great things beyond searching out, and marvellous things beyond number', 9:10).

Even if it were possible to bring God to account in a court of law, Job concludes that his inability to express himself would be his undoing, his own mouth would condemn him (9:20).

But worse than that, Job does not think that God would listen:

'If I summoned him and he answered me,
    I would not believe that he was listening to my voice'
                                                    (9:16).

Job never doubts that God lies behind his trouble: 'If it is not he, then who is it?' (9:24). That is why life seems unfair. *God* seems unfair! That is Job's despair. His world view is falling apart. Life makes no sense. He just cannot understand his situation. The suspicion is growing that God's providence is inherently unjust.

Job feels trapped. He can see no way of escape. There is a hopelessness about his condition that throws him into the darkest despair. He is a pitiful sight at the end of chapter 10. Only the merciless can fail to be touched by his plight.

'There is no arbiter between us,
    who might lay his hand on us both'
                                                    (9:33).

Job cannot see the real battle taking place. He is ignorant of Satan's devices and hence has drawn the conclusion that

God is his enemy, when in truth it is Satan. That is not to say that God is not involved; not at all. God *is* involved, in the deepest possible way. But the situation is far more complicated than Job has imagined. He is caught up in a bigger struggle than he can see.

It is not true that God does not listen to our cries. Nor is it true that God does not care about our plight. He does!

Much later in the story of redemption, God reveals his love for his children in sending his Son 'in the likeness of sinful flesh…' (Rom. 8:3). In the strangling grip of Golgotha, Jesus faced the despairing dilemma of an unfolding providence from which he longed to be free. He was to experience the dereliction of loneliness in a way that no one else had. In the cry of abandonment, when little made sense, when blamelessness met suffering to an unparalleled degree, Jesus was to become for us a sympathizing high priest (Matt. 27:45-46; Heb. 4:15).

Drawing from this aspect of the Saviour's sympathizing role, Isaac Watts could write the hymn that says what Job would have longed to have known:

With joy we meditate the grace
Of our High Priest above;
His heart is made of tenderness,
And overflows with love.

Touched with a sympathy within,
He knows our feeble frame;
He knows what sore temptations mean,
For He has felt the same.

But spotless, innocent, and pure,
The great Redeemer stood,
While Satan's fiery darts He bore,
And did resist to blood.

He in the days of feeble flesh
Poured out His cries and tears;
And, though exalted, feels afresh
What every member bears.

He'll never quench the smoking flax,
But raise it to a flame;
The bruised reed He never breaks,
Nor scorns the meanest name.

Then let our humble faith address
His mercy and His power:
We shall obtain delivering grace
In the distressing hour.

Isaac Watts (1674-1748)

For your journal...

1. When Job asks the question, 'How can a mortal man be right-eous before God?' (9:2, NIV), we argued that this was not a question about what the Bible calls justification. Why is it important to make that point?

2. Is Job correct in thinking that God would not listen to his argument, as he suggests in 9:16? If you were counselling

Job, what would say to him by way of a reply at this point?

3. Meditate on the following verse: 'For we do not have a high priest who is unable to sympathize with our weaknesses, but one who in every respect has been tempted as we are, yet without sin' (Heb. 4:15).

Day 12
The deep things of God

Job 11 – 14

'Though he slay me, I will hope in him;
yet I will argue my ways to his face'
(Job 13:15).

'Man who is born of a woman
is few of days and full of trouble'
(Job 14:1).

Suggested reading: Job 13:13-28

Enter Zophar! He is probably the youngest of the three friends. His contribution is brief and to the point; he doesn't mince his words. God recognizes 'worthless men' (11:11). Job is a 'stupid man' (11:12).

What Job needs to do is simple: he must put iniquity 'far away' (11:14). It is the same recipe as his colleagues delivered earlier: repent of sin and Job will forget his misery, 'you will remember it as waters that have passed away' (11:16). If Job fails to do this, there is a dire warning:

'But the eyes of the wicked will fail;
    all way of escape will be lost to them,
    and their hope is to breathe their last'

(11:20).

Job's response is lengthy, and begins with a note of sarcasm:

'No doubt you are the people,
   and wisdom will die with you'

(12:2),

and moves on quickly to a protestation of how unfair all of this is. Those 'who bring their god in their hand' and 'provoke' him, who dwell in 'tents of robbers' are 'at peace' and 'secure' (12:6), he complains.

Job is challenging the accepted understanding of the world and how it behaves. Good is not always rewarded in this world; nor is evil always punished. And this, as Job insists, is not because God's sovereignty and power have in some way been curtailed. Even though Job cannot fathom it fully, God is sovereign and allows these anomalies to exist regarding good and evil. Animals and birds can tell you that 'the hand of the LORD has done this' (12:9).

Job's friends are 'worthless physicians'. They have argued their case by smearing Job with lies (13:4).

It is at this point, after begging his friends to be silent (13:13), that Job utters one of those memorable lines for which we can but stand back in wonder and admire him:

'Though he slay me, I will hope in him;
   yet I will argue my ways to his face'

(13:15).

Job may not understand what God is doing but he is not about to let go of the truth that he rules. God's sovereignty is an established fact. Whatever the explanation for the way things have turned out, it cannot be at the expense of God's control of the universe. Chaos is not an option that Job is willing to contemplate.

> *If God is not in overall control of all things,*
> *then he is not God!*

What, then, has Job left? What conclusions has he arrived at regarding the nature of the universe? If God is sovereign and goodness goes unrewarded, the only conclusion Job can come to requires him to question God's justice — a conclusion, so far at least, Job is unwilling to consider. Instead he resorts to the hope that after his death, God can raise him up in a different state from the one he now finds himself in:

'If a man dies, shall he live again?
  All the days of my service I would wait,
  till my renewal should come'

(14:14).

This is not a full-blown doctrine of the resurrection of the body, but it does indicate Job's belief in life after death — and he will return to this again.

The Bible often encourages us to look beyond this life, to the world to come, as a way of coping with difficulties. Trouble is what we can expect in this world:

'Man who is born of a woman
  is few of days and full of trouble'

(14:1)

'but man is born to trouble
  as the sparks fly upwards'

(5:7).

Peter warns us of this very principle, that we should never be taken by surprise when we find ourselves the victims of trouble: 'Beloved, do not be surprised at the fiery trial when it comes upon you to test you, as though something strange were happening to you' (1 Peter 4:12). Every disciple of Jesus can expect to engage the implications of cross-bearing. Christians will suffer for no apparent reason. They can find themselves victimized and ridiculed on account of their holiness, rather than as a judgement due to their lack of it. The closer we are to the King, the more likely we are to draw the enemy's fire.

Job is only glimpsing it from a distance here, and only for a brief moment. Quickly the light fades and darkness descends once more. Whatever hope there is lies in the future; the present is torture. His every conscious moment is filled with pain, and Job cannot escape the thought that God is unwilling to do anything about it. Slowly but surely, as water erodes stone, Job's hope fades away (14:19). He is left only with the nightmare of his pain (14:22).

It is a very dark moment for Job. He hasn't stopped believing in God, but he has begun to question God's goodness. God may be powerful, but that power works only to further his distress, not to relieve it.

There is a loneliness to suffering that goes deeper than words. We were created for companionship and mutual support and when these things are gone, the chasm left is vast and daunting. It is the haunting cry that says, 'Nobody understands me. Nobody cares!'

It came home to me in the forlorn words of an otherwise godly and respected man, someone I had looked up to with considerable respect, but who had recently become a widower. Asking if he was now on his way home (following a prayer meeting at the church) he replied, 'It's not my home; it is just the place where I live.'

Some Christians feel like that. Empty. Companionless. It is as though God himself doesn't care. He *may* care, but he does not show it!

Have you ever felt like that? Perhaps you have not uttered it quite as starkly as Job does here; and perhaps you have. It is at such moments that we need to recall our Saviour's words: 'My God, my God, why have you forsaken me?' (Matt. 27:46; Mark 15:34). He, too, experienced the abandonment of a suffering that, to all outward appearances, made no sense at all.

What was it that helped Jesus through the darkness of Gethsemane and the cross? What the book of Hebrews calls, 'the joy that was set before him' (Heb. 12:2). Knowing that heaven awaits every child of God keeps us going through the darkest periods.

> In heavenly love abiding,
> No change my heart shall fear;
> And safe in such confiding,
> For nothing changes here:
> The storm may roar without me,
> My heart may low be laid;
> But God is round about me,
> And can I be dismayed?
>
> Anna L. Waring (1820-1910)

For your journal...

1. At various points in the book of Job there seems to be a sudden change in his emotional response. Take, for example, the words of Job 13:15: 'Though he slay me, I will hope in him,' followed as they are at verse 24 by the words, 'Why do you hide your face and count me as your enemy?' How do you explain this?

2. Is the view, as Job expresses it, that our lives are 'full of trouble' (14:1) unnecessarily pessimistic? Can you think of some balancing truths?

3. Meditate on the words of our Saviour: 'Why have you forsaken me?' (Matt. 27:46). What bearing, if any, do they have on Job's predicament?

Day 13
A witness in heaven

Job 15 – 17

'Even now, behold, my witness is in heaven,
and he who testifies for me is on high.
My friends scorn me;
my eye pours out tears to God'
(Job 16:19-20).

Suggested reading: Job 16:16-22

Those who have suffered great loss will tell you that they coped when the trial first came. It is when it refuses to go away that the trouble begins. 'My pain is not assuaged' (16:6). 'My spirit is broken' (17:1).

Job has begun to think the unthinkable. He has begun to think that God has become his enemy — that God has been his enemy all along!

Surely now God has worn me out;
   he has made desolate all my company.
And he has shrivelled me up,
   which is a witness against me,
and my leanness has risen up against me;
   it testifies to my face.

He has torn me in his wrath and hated me;
    he has gnashed his teeth at me;
my adversary sharpens his eyes against me'

(16:7-9).

God's eyes have burnt holes in him. He feels torn to shreds. God is his foe!

Job is not unaware that others are involved, for example 'the wicked' (16:11). Even knowing that much does not alleviate the problem entirely. The ultimate problem for Job is God himself. How can he appeal for justice when the highest source of judgement and arbitration appears unscrupulous and crooked?

This, of course, is Satan's doing, but Job does not understand it yet. Satan always wants to draw attention away from himself by making God and his ways appear malevolent, unprincipled *and unjust.* This has been a stratagem of his from the very start, and we must familiarize ourselves with it (cf. Eph. 6:11).

If we cannot trust God, whom can we trust?

All that is left is a form of nihilism and despair. There is nowhere to turn and find relief. All sources of help are closed. There is only emptiness and a sense of futility.

And yet, it is to God — this God who appears so unfair — that Job continually turns. 'My eye pours out tears to God' (16:20).

He may be in despair, he may be angry, he may feel abandoned and victimized; but he is letting God know just what he thinks, what *he feels*! And here, yes, just here, lie the seeds of his eventual recovery. For as sure as day follows night, his

recovery will stem from his communion with God, troubled as
that now is. It is the maxim of that well-known hymn by Joseph
Scriven, 'What a Friend we have in Jesus':

> Have we trials and temptations?
> Is there trouble anywhere?
> We should never be discouraged:
> Take it to the Lord in prayer.

God may appear silent at this moment, and Job may be drawing all the wrong conclusions about his motives and goals; but
he insists that the answer to it all lies with God. Yet the silence
of God is deafening. For now, Job has to contend with these
'miserable comforters' and their 'long-winded speeches' (16:1).

'I know that my Redeemer lives…' (19:25) is a verse that
is well known to most of us. George Frederick Handel made it
all the more familiar in his oratorio, *Messiah*. Interestingly,
Job has already said something that relates to this.

> 'There is no arbiter between us,
>   who might lay his hand on us both'
>
>   (9:33).

In today's reading, he says something similar:

> 'Even now, behold, my witness is in heaven,
>   and he who testifies for me is on high'
>
>   (16:19).

Job is absolutely certain that in heaven there is a 'witness',
one who argues Job's case as someone might do for his friend
(16:20-21).

Who is this arbitrator, intercessor, witness, redeemer? Ultimately it is Jesus, of course. But Job is not aware of that here. What he sees is only a faint glimpse. It is as though he was jumping up in front of a high wall, catching only the briefest glance of what lies on the other side before landing again.

And what he sees is quickly forgotten. It fails to take hold. Despair once more descends and clouds his vision. Job's spirit 'is broken' (17:1). He is the object of scorn ('a byword' 17:6). His dreams are shattered (17:11). There is only one certainty now: death! (17:16).

Are you surprised by the suddenness of Job's mood changes? He moves from hope to despair in a few verses. Rapidly the darkness falls and engulfs him.

Anyone who has suffered a crippling sickness, or the effects of bereavement, knows how these things can occur. Hope and confidence are based on the flimsiest of things and are soon dissipated. Cancer patients gain and lose confidence in response to pain, or an overly frank discussion on the state of their disease.

Broken! That is how Job feels. Like a useless branch lying beside a tree, severed from its source of life and energy — fit for nothing except firewood.

Without the reassurances of the promises of Scripture (something Job did not possess), we too would have no recourse to confidence in the purposes of God. Promises such as:

'He gives power to the faint,
    and to him who has no might he increases strength'
                                                    (Isa. 40:29).

'A bruised reed he will not break,
   and a faintly burning wick he will not quench;
   he will faithfully bring forth justice'
(Isa. 42:3; cf. Matt. 12:20).

'I will never leave you nor forsake you'
(Heb. 13:5).

For your journal...

1. At no point does Job acknowledge the work of Satan. He does not seem to know of his existence. How much does Satan's involvement, as we are told about it in the opening chapters, affect the situation? Does this 'solve' the problem of pain, or not?

2. What does Job mean by his 'witness ... in heaven' (16:19)? Does Revelation 1:5 help to give us a greater understanding of the reference?

3. Job calls his friends 'miserable comforters' (16:2). Is this fair, do you think?

Day 14
My Redeemer lives

Job 18 – 19

'For I know that my Redeemer lives,
and at the last he will stand upon the earth.
And after my skin has been thus destroyed,
yet in my flesh I shall see God,
whom I shall see for myself,
and my eyes shall behold, and not another.
My heart faints within me!'
(Job 19:25-27).

Suggested reading: Job 19:23-29

In chapter 19, Job is responding to another of Bildad's speeches (Job 18). We might call this contribution by Bildad, *The Dwellings of the Wicked*, so long as we appreciate that for Bildad, Job is the principal character; he is the wicked one!

Bildad will have nothing to do with Job's claim of innocence. That would involve a reversal of his entire moral system (18:4). The world as he knows it works according to very definite principles: sin is punished and goodness is rewarded. Suffering is always chastisement because you get what you deserve in this life, no more and no less.

Bildad is quite the preacher! His use of metaphor, simile and illustration makes his oratory gripping. The wicked are those in whose homes the lamp has gone out and there is no welcoming light to guide the traveller home (18:5). The light had gone out in Job's home.

Bildad pictures an old man shuffling along, stumbling over obstacles in the way, and falling down (v. 7). He is caught in a trap, a noose, a snare, a mesh, a net, and there is no escape (vv. 8-10). Terrors, calamity and disaster overtake him (vv. 11-12). Disease eats up his flesh (v. 13). With a play on words, Bildad takes the common name for one of the Canaanite gods, *Mot*, and turns it into the Hebrew word for 'death', *mawot*, suggesting that an emissary comes and marches him off, as in some police-state, to 'the King of Terrors' (v. 14). Fire and destruction devastate his home (v. 15).

This is quite a sermon! And it is unbelievably cruel. It ends with a picture of this wicked man with 'no posterity or progeny among his people, and no survivor where he used to live' (v. 19). Given that Job has lost all ten of his children, this must have been a savage blow for him to hear from his 'friend'.

Furthermore, the sermon ends:

'Surely such are the dwellings of the unrighteous,
    such is the place of him who knows not God'

(v. 21).

This has been a sermon *about Job*! Job is the most wicked man imaginable and his suffering is proof of it.

With friends like this, who needs enemies?

Job's response is both predictable and understandable. He feels abandoned and rejected.

> *Rejected by his counsellors.* Their attacks have been shameless (19:3).
> *Rejected by his friends.* His wife, little boys, his intimate friends … all of them 'have turned against me' (19:19).
> *Rejected by God!* '…God has put me in the wrong' (19:6).

It is this last thought that upsets him the most. What happens when *God abandons us and becomes our enemy?* What then? The Hebrew word translated 'wrong' above (19:6) is the verb 'to pervert'. Thus, justice has been perverted. 'The hand of God has struck me' (19:21, NIV).

If Bildad can use graphic pictures, so can Job. Job imagines himself caught in a net (v. 6), set up by thugs and abandoned (v. 7), unable to get home (v. 8), humiliated as a prince by some alien king (v. 9), forced into single-handed combat (v. 11), surrounded by besieging armies (v. 12), *without hope* (v. 10).

Can a Christian feel like this? It is an important question. For many people, such melancholy and gloom seems to be out of keeping with true spirituality.

Robert Davis, a minister suffering the initial stages of Alzheimer's Disease, wrote down his responses and feelings while he still remembered them. He described his condition at one time, knowing what lay before him, as 'a combination of medical, psychological, mental and spiritual changes that tossed me like a cork in the sea'.[1]

This is Job. He has not stopped believing in God; it's just that God does not seem to be answering him. It is similar to

the account in Mark 5 when Jairus' daughter is sick and he
asks Jesus for help, only to find that Jesus gets sidetracked
with a woman who has another urgent problem. By the time
Jesus comes back to Jairus, it is too late; the girl is dead. 'Don't
be afraid, but believe,' Jesus says. Like Jairus, Job is being asked
to believe when everything is pointing in the opposite
direction.

This is why Job needs a mediator. Since Job himself cannot
speak to God and plead his case (because God does not appear
to be listening), he needs someone to do it for him, someone
with greater ability. Tempting as it is to see in this expression
the need for someone to forgive us our sins before we can
enter God's presence, this is not Job's plea here. It is not so
much a Saviour that Job is asking for (though Job would not
have denied that he needed one); rather, what Job needs is an
arbitrator, someone to defend him before God.

The Hebrew word, translated 'mediator' here, is an interesting one. It is the word that describes Boaz, for example, in
the story of Naomi and Ruth. Boaz was the member of the
family, the kinsman, whose role it was to defend the honour
of the family in times of trouble and seek justice and redress.
He was under obligation to care for, even marry, Ruth, the
wife of his deceased relative. Job is saying something similar
here. He is confident that such a person exists to plead his
case before God.

We may pour into this more than perhaps Job could see.
Jesus ever lives to intercede for us (Heb. 7:25). He helps us
(Heb. 2:18). He sympathizes (Heb. 4:15). And this is Job's
confidence. Perhaps he spoke beyond his own comprehen-
sion. He has no certainty that he will be alive to see the result
of his Redeemer's work on his behalf. 'At the last he will stand

upon the earth,' he says (Job 19:25), suggesting (since the Hebrew word for earth can also mean 'dust') that even if Job dies, his Redeemer will stand in triumph over his 'dust' and proclaim his case and validate him before God.

And then, Job announces a belief in his future resurrection.

'And after my skin has been thus destroyed,
  yet in my flesh I shall see God,
 whom I shall see for myself,
  and my eyes shall behold, and not another.
  My heart faints within me!'

(19:26-27).

How can this be after such words of gloom and despair? Only those who have never been where Job has been will ask this question. Those who have trod this path will know how suddenly moods can swing, how despair can be answered by sudden moments of light and hope, only to sink back again to darkness and gloom. We are fearfully and wonderfully made!

Job's momentary relief came as he considered the *total* picture — one that transcends the boundaries of this world. Here there may be no justice; but in the world to come there certainly will be.

Here, there may be a death;
  there, in the world to come there will be life.
Here, there may be a cross to carry;
  there, in the world to come, there will be victory.

Believe it!

For your journal...

1. What does Job mean when he says, 'God has put me in the wrong' (19:6)? To what extent would you reprove him for saying this?

2. What interpretation of the famous passage, 'I know that my Redeemer lives' (19:25-27) did this chapter give? Do you agree with it?

3. To what extent do you think that our evaluation of our circumstances is necessarily distorted by the fact that we have only a partial knowledge of things?

Day 15
Refined gold

Job 21 – 24

'I have treasured the words of his mouth
more than my portion of food'
(Job 23:12).

Suggested reading: Job 23:1-12

These words sound a little too strong for some commentators. Some think that Job, like Ophelia in Shakespeare's *Hamlet*, protests too much. 'I have not departed from the commandment of his lips,' Job insists, adding, 'I have treasured the words of his mouth more than my portion of food. But he is unchangeable, and who can turn him back?' (23:12-13).

It is tempting to agree with these commentators. Maintaining a consistent line of defence on Job's behalf involves a suspicion at times that no one is *that* innocent! To yield to such a notion is, of course, to deny the testimony given of Job's character in the opening prologue to the book of Job — a testimony underlined by the fact that it is made by God himself! Job's suffering does not have anything to do with his personal sin and any suspicion we may entertain that Job has made his case too often and too assertively falls into the trap of siding with Job's friends! No, Job is 'innocent', and any explanation of his suffering must not yield half way through the book to a line of argument that makes the cogency of the whole story unsafe.

This protest by Job has emerged in response to Eliphaz's no-holds-barred insistence that Job's evil is 'abundant' (22:5). Zophar had spoken before him, saying much the same thing — implying that Job was 'wicked' and 'godless' (20:5). According to Zophar, Job can expect 'the heavens' to 'reveal his iniquity' and 'the earth' to 'rise up against him' (20:27).

Now it is Eliphaz' turn, and he has even found time to list a string of shortcomings on Job's part, including his treatment of widows and orphans (22:9).

According to Eliphaz, Job has followed the path of those who think that they can sin and get away with it, saying, 'What can the Almighty do to us?' (22:17). Job's sin is high-handed and flagrant. He has resisted God and is paying the price for it. He is treading the path that evil men have taken (v. 15) and they are now dead, 'snatched away before their time' (v. 16).

What Job must do is submit to God and 'be at peace' (v. 21). Restoration is sure to follow a genuine repentance on Job's part (v. 23). This is the way to a renewed sense of delight in God.

It sounds like a broken record, doesn't it? These men have nothing new to say. Their words may sound eloquent and, by turns, sophisticated; but, in reality, it is the same old song that they are singing, and it is sounding very stale indeed. They are heedless to the thought that they might just be wrong! That notion does not seem to register with them at all. They are bent on getting their point across, no matter how often they have to say it.

The power of such an onslaught is bound to have an affect on the stoutest mind, even on the best of days. In Job's weakened condition it is more than he can bear. God's hand lies heavily upon him (23:2) and, what is more, God cannot be found!

There are days when our prayers fail to ascend, or so it seems to us. Our words fall like dead birds from the sky. All Job desires is a day in court with God to argue his case, to ask for mercy, to be given *some sort of explanation*. Is that too much to ask? Doesn't God care enough to answer a simple prayer like that? It is not beyond his power to resolve, in an instant. The silence is deafening.

'Oh, that I knew where I might find him,
   that I might come even to his seat!...
'Behold, I go forwards, but he is not there,
   and backwards, but I do not perceive him;
on the left hand when he is working, I do not behold him;
   he turns to the right hand, but I do not see him'
(23:3, 8-9).

Is it really too much to ask that as a child of God we may have an audience with him when we please? Isn't that what being 'fellow citizens with the saints and members of the household of God' means (Eph. 2:19)? But Job has found no such audience. The thought occurs to Job that there might be something arbitrary about the way God does things.

It is a terrifying thought that there might be something capricious about God's ways. Job admits that it really frightens him! 'The Almighty has terrified me,' he says (23:15-16).

Yet Job will not be silenced! That is what Job's perseverance means! God may be silent. God may seem to be ignoring

him; but Job will not give up. He refuses to lie down and be
silent:

> 'yet I am not silenced because of the darkness,
>   nor because thick darkness covers my face'
>
>   (23:17).

Out of this darkness arises a thought that Job hardly knows
he has uttered. He makes nothing of it, and no sooner has it
emerged than a sea of troubles drowns it out. But a truth has
emerged, sharper and more eloquent than anything that he
has uttered so far. It is the heart of the book. It is a key that
unlocks his plight, if only he had realized it. Like a deer frozen
in the headlights it shines in all its beauty, but all Job can see
is the impending catastrophe if it does not move out of the
way.
What is it?

> 'But he knows the way that I take;
>   when he has tried me, I shall come out as gold'
>
>   (23:10).

We need to be careful as to how we interpret these words.
It is essential that we see them in the context of the argument
of the book of Job. Frequently they are taken to mean that
God purges away our sins, as dross is removed in a refining
process, by means of trials. That is true, but it is not the truth
being taught here. Job is not admitting to any sin that may
explain his trial. The 'gold' that Job has in mind is his argument, his 'good case', which, he has insisted from the beginning, has merit.

Seen in that light, Job's words take on a very different twist. His confidence is not his purification so much as his vindication! God will show these friends of his that he has been right all along! Arrogant though that sounds, Job is correct! God has told us so in the very opening lines of the book.

What this says is very important. God's truth will be vindicated in the end. Satan will not be able to rob God of his glory. Job is a child of God and nothing Satan does can take that away. Job is not going to turn and curse God. He will come forth as gold. It may look entirely unbelievable at present, but such is the providence of God.

> *Its truth may lie hidden, but we are to rest assured that it will emerge victorious.*

Self-serving? It may appear that way, but it isn't. Job will utter some things that he will regret, but this is not one of them. What keeps him going through the darkness of his despair is the hope, no, the certainty, that God is righteous. And far from being a threat, that is his anchor amidst the storm. Is it yours? It certainly was the psalmist's:

'Vindicate me, O LORD,
    for I have walked in my integrity,
    and I have trusted in the LORD without wavering'

(26:1).

'Vindicate me, O LORD, my God,
    according to your righteousness,
    and let them not rejoice over me!'

(35:24).

'Vindicate me, O God, and defend my cause
      against an ungodly people,
from the deceitful and unjust man
      deliver me!'

(43:1).

'O God, save me, by your name,
      and vindicate me by your might'

(54:1).

For your journal...

1. To what extent is it important to maintain a consistent defence of Job's plea of innocence as we continue to study the book of Job?

2. How far can we *demand* of God an answer to our questions about the way things are (providence)? Do we have some inalienable rights when it comes to our understanding of what God may be doing? How do you think Philippians 2:5-11 relates to this issue?

3. Imagine the loneliness Job felt when he uttered the words, 'Oh, that I knew where I might find him' (23:3). Elisabeth Elliot, speaking of loneliness, has written: 'Offer it up — thank God for the transformability of the problem you don't want, but still have. Thank God for his power that can take the worst and make it into the best.' Reflect on how this may apply to situations in your own life.

Day 16
Worm theology

Job 25

'Behold, even the moon is not bright,
and the stars are not pure in his eyes;
how much less man, who is a maggot,
and the son of man, who is a worm!'
(Job 25:5-6).

Suggested reading: Job 25:1-6

One of the things that we can easily get wrong about these so-called friends of Job is that what they have to say is perfectly orthodox. These are not rank heretics, spouting profanity and error at every turn. On the contrary, they have a profound sense of God's majesty and greatness. Theirs is no feeble, ineffective God, unable to help Job in his predicament. As Bildad now exclaims: 'Dominion and fear are with God' (25:1).

The problem with so much modern theology, whether it be liberal or evangelical, is that it portrays a God who is weak and fragile. On the one hand, we have those who think the future is 'open' to God and not determined in any way; and on the other, we have those who insist that God cannot possibly be involved in pain and suffering. Bildad and his companions will have none of this.

Bildad has actually run out of steam! His final contribution is only six verses in length. And Zophar (whose turn would follow) does not say anything at all. They have, after all, been repeating themselves. They have nothing new to say. Bildad's final contribution is a not-so-eloquent espousal of 'worm theology'.

'Behold, even the moon is not bright,
　　and the stars are not pure in his eyes;
how much less man, who is a maggot,
　　and the son of man, who is a worm!'

(vv. 5-6).

Two issues emerge here that are worth noting. One has to do with Bildad's understanding of the righteousness of God. The other concerns his assessment of Job and fallen men and women in general.

According to Bildad, even 'the stars are not pure in his eyes' (v. 5). For all the beauty of the created world (and each of us has a favourite location that takes our breath away), the world is fallen and subject to the curse pronounced in Genesis 3:17-18: 'Cursed is the ground ... thorns and thistles it shall bring forth.' The universe has been 'subjected to futility' (Rom. 8:20).

That may be difficult to believe when we view a particular landscape. How can inanimate objects be considered as impure? It is important to distinguish what the Bible teaches at this point from speculative philosophy. Matter itself, the stuff of the universe, is not *in itself* sinful. Various theologies have taught over the centuries that salvation consists in being released from the 'prison' of materialism. Examples vary considerably, but it was the view taught by Tatian, a second-century pupil of Justin Martyr who abandoned Christianity and became an Encratitic Gnostic, regarding matter as evil. On another level, it led Augustine to a view of sexuality that was unbiblical and unhealthy.

It is not that matter is itself inherently sinful, but that matter has been subjected to futility (death, disease, distress) by reason of sin's entrance into the world. The world that God created was inherently 'good' (Gen. 1: 4, 10, 12, 18, 21, 25), even 'very good' (v. 31). But the world no longer serves the end for which it was created. The laws of thermodynamics now contain a destructive principle that manifests the universe's frustration rather than concord.

Even Calvin faltered here. Several times in his 159 sermons on the book of Job Calvin speculates that God's righteousness is such that even created matter itself is to be regarded as impure. Calvin's point of departure begins in his understanding of what is said in the opening chapters of Job, that even the angels are 'charged with error' (4:18). Calvin understands this to be said of unfallen angels. That brings him to a view that there exists a righteousness in God which surpasses the righteousness which he has revealed to us in his law. The point he is making is that even if Job were to be pure in terms of his obedience to the law, he remains impure to the eyes of God whose righteousness exceeds anything that can be achieved by mere obedience. The issues involved here are complex, and it leads Calvin in the end to disregard Job's 'good case' that he is innocent. Nobody, not even the unfallen angels, are pure in God's sight.

Taking Job 4:18 to refer to *fallen* angels removes this line of interpretation entirely. Then, Bildad's point is, on one level, well made. How can anyone claim purity in God's sight when the creation itself is fallen? Simply by being made of the material stuff of the universe Job is impure in God's sight. No one, not even Job, can claim impurity before God.

The point is well made. It sounds evangelical and biblical. But Bildad is not finished. Not only is God's righteousness such that everything falls short by comparison; but also man, Job in particular, is fallen. More than that, Job is a 'maggot' and a 'worm' by comparison (25:6).

There has been a reaction of late to what is sometimes referred to as 'worm theology'. In part, it has reacted to such expressions as the one in Isaac Watts's hymn, 'Alas! And did my Saviour Bleed':

Alas! and did my Saviour bleed
And did my Sovereign die?
Would He devote that sacred head
For such a worm as I?

The source I used for this hymn had actually substituted 'For sinners such as I?' in place of the final line!

Part of the problem — and, despite what we might now say, it *is* a problem — is that such an assessment of our condition (that we are worms) can seriously damage a proper sense of self-esteem. The expression 'self-esteem' is a 'buzz' word likely to evoke immediate reactions, but psychological damage results from a low self-esteem that is not accompanied by the biblical balance of what the Bible teaches about our being made in the image of God.

The stamp of the divine rests upon us no matter how sinful we are, and Christians need the constant reminder that we are sons of God (Gal. 3:26).

Nevertheless, the Bible does use the expression 'worm' (Ps. 22:6; Isa. 41:14) even if it is Bildad who uses it here. Hostility towards this term is mainly a reaction against the Bible's view of our depravity, but some caution needs to be expressed. Care needs to be taken when describing a believer as a 'worm' having no great significance and usefulness. Worms and sin are not easily related, and it is hard not to convey a sense of insignificance to the concept when used of a human being. The Bible insists that man bears God's image in a way that a worm does not. As far as Bildad is concerned, it is one more nail in Job's coffin, consigning this influential and important man to the scrap heap of society.

As a piece of counselling, this really is inept. Do not beat a man when he is down, they used to say, but Bildad has no such compunction. Jesus, one imagines, would not have treated Job this way, no matter what view of our innate depravity he had.

Every time I read these contributions of Job's friends, I am driven to thank God that Jesus' counsel is of a different kind. The 'bruised reed he will not break' (Matt. 12:20) — he will *not* break!

For your journal...

1. How might Isaiah 41:14, 'Fear not, you worm Jacob, you men of Israel! I am the one who helps you, declares the LORD; your Redeemer is the Holy One of Israel' be of help to us in countering Bildad's use of 'worm theology'?

2. In what ways do the issues of 'self-esteem' and a biblical theology of sin relate and conflict? Do you know how these may balance in your own life?

3. Reflect on the words engraved on the tombstone of William Carey (1761 – 1834):

William Carey
Born August 17th, 1761
Died June 1834
A wretched, poor and helpless worm,
on Thy kind arms I fall.

Day 17
Justice denied

Job 26 - 27

'God ... has taken away my right
... the Almighty ... has made my soul bitter'
(Job 27:2).

Suggested reading: Job 27:1-8

'Far be it from me to say that you are right; till I die I will not put away my integrity from me' (Job 27:5).

These are Job's final words to his friends. He goes on: 'I hold fast my righteousness and will not let it go; my heart does not reproach me for any of my days' (v. 6). And all of this, after a breathtaking chapter extolling the majesty of God (26:1-14)!

Job may well be confident of the rightness of his position, but only at the expense of seriously damaging his understanding of God's character. The Almighty 'has made my soul bitter', he protests (27:2). Justice has been denied him. His day in court has not materialized. To all intents and purposes, God's integrity is suspect.

Job has had enough. His friends have accused him of gross wickedness.

Job retaliates. He engages in what we sometimes refer to as an *imprecation*. Since his friends have accused him of wickedness, he now calls upon them to be judged as the wicked deserve.

'Let my enemy be as the wicked,
     and let him who rises up
          against me be as the unrighteous'

(27:7).

Before we judge Job too harshly here, we need to recall that pain can sometimes make us lash out at those we love. Most of us would acknowledge that we often say things in a crisis that we would otherwise regret. Nor is Job the only one to do this (for a few 'no-holds-barred' examples, see Neh. 4:4-5; Ps. 109:6-15; 139:7-8; Jer. 18:21-23; 1 Cor. 16:22).

What are we to make of them? Some have attempted to explain them as poetic hyperbole (e.g. Derek Kidner). Matthew Henry saw them as predictions of doom rather than personal prayers for destruction. And others have seen these as something that belong to the Old Testament, to the days of incomplete revelation (e.g. Alexander MacClaren).

C. S. Lewis, along with many others, went further and saw them as carnal, uninspired expressions of personal vindictiveness, something entirely unworthy of a Christian to utter in any context. In his book, *Reflections on the Psalms*, he speaks of the imprecatory psalms as 'the refinement of malice', 'diabolical', and 'contemptible'. He adds: 'In some of the psalms the spirit of hatred which strikes us in the face is like the heat from a furnace mouth.' Again, 'We must not either try to explain them away or to yield for one moment to the idea that, because it comes in the Bible, all this vindictive hatred must somehow be good and pious. We must face both facts squarely. The hatred is there — festering, gloating, undisguised — and also we should be wicked if we in any way condoned or approved it.'[1]

The view that somehow these expressions belong to the Old Testament is ruled out by the fact that Paul utters an imprecation as blatant as any other: 'If anyone has no love for the Lord, let him be accursed. Our Lord, come!' (1 Cor. 16:22). For this reason, many evangelical and reformed commentators have maintained that these imprecations identify a level of maturity rather than impiety on the part of those who utter them. There are situations where an imprecation is the right thing to utter.

In order to prevent an imprecation from becoming an expression of personal revenge (something which is very difficult to do) some limits need to be established. Calvin Beisner, in a wonderfully helpful commentary on some of the psalms, suggests three limits on the use of imprecatory prayer.

1. The curses must be firmly rooted in God's standard of righteousness and judgement, not in our own petty opinions or hurt pride.

2. The imprecations must be offered only for God's glory, not our own.

3. Cursing prayer must be offered only in the utmost personal humility and after merciless self-examination, for it amounts to pronouncing God's judgement.[2]

These limitations are designed to prevent us from self-righteously asserting our own opinions of justice and

righteousness as the infallible decree of God. John Calvin
shows much wisdom in this area:

> And as we cannot distinguish between the elect and
> the reprobate, it is our duty to pray for all who trouble
> us; to desire the salvation of all men; and even to be
> careful for the welfare of every individual. At the same
> time, if our hearts are pure and peaceful, this will not
> prevent us from freely appealing to God's judgement,
> that he may cut off the finally impenitent.[3]

Was Job right to say what he did? It is impossible for us to
judge Job's heart here. What were his precise motivations in
uttering these words? It is impossible for us to discern. In theory,
however, Job's prayer reflects no more than the desire that
God's justice be applied to those who remain enemies of God.
Were his friends enemies of God? They were certainly wrong
in their assessment of Job, just as they were wrong in their
application of theology. But does this make them enemies?
Perhaps not. We can be wrong about something and still be
sincere in our motives. Job's friends were inept, even uncaring;
but they desired that Job's relationship with God be put on a
better footing than it currently seemed to be.

These are the words of a broken spirit, one who is con-
vinced that he has been denied justice (27:1). And in such
circumstances it is all too easy to cross the line.

These are dark passages that disturb us deeply when we
read them, as we suspect that we, too, have thought *and said*
such things. 'Be angry and do not sin' (Eph. 4:26) has to be
one of the most difficult commandments to obey! When our
emotions are frayed, we are at the mercy of satanic forces!

Somewhere in all of this, Job crosses the line. Later, he confesses to having spoken foolishly. And when he does, he will receive the forgiveness of God.

There is forgiveness! A deep, lasting forgiveness that holds no grudges! *Blessed Jesus!*

For your journal...

1. Think through the issue of retribution for a moment. We noted Job's desire in 27:7 that his enemies be regarded as 'unrighteous'. How does this square with such passages as 'Bless those who curse you, pray for those who abuse you' (Luke 6:28)?

2. How can anger be justified? When does anger become a sin? How does the following passage help us here: 'Be angry and do not sin; do not let the sun go down on your anger' (Eph. 4:26)?

3. Jonah was angry with God because of a plant (Jonah 4:9). Can we ever be justified in feeling angry with God? Reflect on ways that we get angry at God's providence.

Day 18
Mining for wisdom

Job 28

'From where, then, does wisdom come?
And where is the place of understanding?'
(Job 28:20).

Suggested reading: Job 28:1-11

The book of Job is classified as 'wisdom' literature, which identifies it as having a very particular style and purpose. The word 'wisdom' in Scripture is not used in the same way as we would use it in our everyday conversation. Bible wisdom is not interested in training someone for a Phi Beta Kappa scholarship; rather, it is concerned with how we may live our lives as God's children in a way that best accomplishes the purposes he has for us. 'Wisdom' books in the Bible are always very practical in nature.

There is a hymn, a verse of which reads as follows:

He formed the stars, those heav'nly flames,
He counts their numbers, calls their names;
His wisdom's vast, and knows no bound,
A deep where all our thoughts are drowned.[1]

This is Isaac Watts' rendition of a part of Psalm 147. 'His wisdom's vast, and knows no bounds...' is the theme of one particular chapter in Job, which we now consider; but, in effect, it is the theme of the entire book of Job.

'From where, then, does wisdom come?
And where is the place of understanding?'

(28:20).

Where can wisdom be found? It is an important question at any time, but to a man who feels that life is unfair and justice is hard to get, this cry seems all the more poignant.

The chapter has all the look and feel of a poem about it, written perhaps independently of the flow of debate between Job and his friends. One fine commentary on Job, for example, calls this chapter an 'Interlude'. It seems to be what we might call a 'time-out' reflection on the nature and sources of wisdom.

Job's friends have run out of steam. Their voices, bitter and biting, have now fallen silent. Job is left to himself to reflect and ponder on one of the great themes of life. And his conclusion? That wisdom is to be found in the fear of the Lord. The full text is worth citing, for it encapsulates the message of the book of Job in one verse!

'The fear of the Lord, that is wisdom,
And to turn away from evil is understanding'

(28:28).

This had been Job's understanding of the way life is to be lived, but it had landed him in deep trouble. That is why in the opening verses of the next chapter we find him longing for the days when this rule of life seemed to bring God's discernible blessing. It all seems to have gone terribly wrong. His understanding of the way God works in this world seems to have been turned upside down. The world — his life, *God's providence* — doesn't seem to make any sense!

What can we expect if we commit ourselves to a life of godliness? If we 'shun evil' as Job has been doing, and is determined to continue to do, what then? Job's friends have a ready answer: righteousness leads to a life that is free from suffering. Invariably, pain is punishment for disobedience.

But Job is discovering that the wisdom of God is more complicated than that. Neat, packaged solutions, which the counsellors offered, are woefully inadequate as an explanation for all of life's issues. What Job comes to appreciate here — appreciate, perhaps, more in his head than his heart — is one of the most profound things we can ever discover. It is a key to life itself — the life of God within the soul of man. It will take a few chapters and a revelation of God to move Job's heart into submission; but right here, in chapter 28, Job begins to understand what the real issue is all about.

Understanding is the first step to discipleship.

It all boils down to what we *think*. Our mind matters. Our world and life view, as the expression goes, commits us to a certain way of life. It is time for Job to sit and ponder the ultimate realities of life in this world.

Does life have any meaning? Or is life, after all, meaningless? For all the effort and labour we put into it, we are all of us, rich and poor alike, subject to the Great Leveller — the moment when we are marched off to meet death, 'the king of terrors' (Job 18:14). Einstein, Dostoevsky, Shakespeare,

Beethoven… it doesn't matter who we are, or what we have
been — this is what awaits us all.

This is the perspective of the preacher in the book of
Ecclesiastes when he thinks about life: 'Vanity of vanities, says
the Preacher; all is vanity' (12:8). Is there really no meaning
to life? Is the sceptic right, after all? Is life basically unfair? Is
there no order, no structure, no universal law, no truth? You
live and then you die, so you had better make the most of it.
It's each man for himself. You may show kindness and love,
but, in the end, it will make no difference. Is this how it is?

'In my vain life I have seen everything. There is a righteous man who perishes in his righteousness, and there
is a wicked man who prolongs his life in his evildoing'
(Eccles. 7:15).

Epicures was right: 'Let us eat and drink, for tomorrow we
die.' As Robert Herrick put it:

Gather ye rosebuds while ye may,
Old Time is still a-flying
And this same flower that smiles to-day
To-morrow will be dying.[2]

Job is not prepared to accept that life is meaningless. That
is what he means when he says in 27:6: 'I hold fast my righteousness and will not let it go; my heart does not reproach me
for any of my days.' As we have said before, that sounds terribly self-righteous, doesn't it? We would be tempted to say, 'No
one is perfect, not even you, Job!' But, tempting as this may
be, that would be to misunderstand this book, and capitulate
to the theological world view of Job's friends. Job does indeed

have a good case; God has told us so. Job is not about to turn his understanding of the world and the way God works in creation and grace upside down just because his friends keep insisting that he is wrong. There is wisdom somewhere, but where?

Job imagines a mining expedition. The opening verses of this chapter give us a fascinating glimpse into ancient mining techniques. It describes the way silver and gold and precious gems are extracted from the depths of the earth where no creature apart from man has ever been (28:1-11). Things regarded as precious have a source that can be accessed, even if it involves great pain and arduous struggle. They may not yield their beauty easily, but they are obtainable. The ancients could dig great tunnels deep into the surface of the earth, but finding wisdom is another thing entirely. Where can I find it?

Can it be bought? Can I write a cheque and buy wisdom? Can I sign up for a course at one of the world's greatest universities and get wisdom? Yes, to some degree, that is possible. And yet, as the preacher complains in Ecclesiastes, the intelligent are also destitute of true wisdom. They may have intellectual knowledge, but they are unhappy. They fail to find the source of all true meaning and purpose.

> 'I devoted myself to study and to explore by wisdom all
> that is done under heaven … all of them are meaning-
> less, a chasing after the wind'
> (Eccles. 1:13-14, NIV).

One of the most disturbing features of almost any modern university where the brightest students are found is that you will also observe some of the most offensive and hope-*less* graffiti.

Man does not comprehend its worth;
it cannot be found in the land of the living.
The deep says, 'It is not in me';
the sea says, 'It is not with me.'
It cannot be bought with the finest gold,
nor can its price be weighed in silver...
It is hidden from the eyes of every living thing,
concealed even from the birds of the air
                                    (28:13-15, 21, NIV).

For all of man's achievements and abilities, he cannot answer Job's great question about the meaning and purpose of a righteous man who suffers. Nothing in this world can explain that. The answer to life's great questions cannot be discerned by man alone. He may fly to the moon, and explore the double-helix structure of DNA and map the human genome; he may compose a sublime symphony like Beethoven's Ninth or Mahler's Ninth; he may write poetry like Keats or Shelley; he may paint like Rembrandt or Titian; but can he find wisdom — the kind of wisdom that speaks of ultimate truth and reality? He cannot! He cannot find the wisdom of God.

The answer is not completely negative. There is a 'rumour' of wisdom that is discernible in this world (cf. 28:22). The world reflects something of the wisdom of God, but Job is concerned about something deeper than that. He says:

'God understands the way to it,
and he knows its place.
For he looks to the ends of the earth
and sees everything under the heavens'
                                    (28:23-24).

The answer to Job's question, in the ultimate sense, is Jesus Christ! He is 'the wisdom of God' (1 Cor. 1:24). It is in fellowship with Jesus Christ that everything begins to make sense. And even if it doesn't *make sense*, knowing him assures me that everything makes sense *to him* if not to me. And that is all that matters in the end.

For your journal...

1. How might 'wisdom literature', like the book of Job, answer questions differently from, say, Paul's letters? What kind of things do you expect the book of Job to say, knowing that it is classified as a 'wisdom' book?

2. Meditate on the following words of Paul and ask yourself what bearing they might have on Job 28: 'He is the source of your life in Christ Jesus, whom God made our wisdom and our righteousness and sanctification and redemption' (1 Cor. 1:30).

3. Can you think of some way in which our *understanding* can govern our emotional and spiritual response?

Day 19
The fear of God

Job 28

*'Behold, the fear of the Lord, that is wisdom,
and to turn away from evil is understanding'
(Job 28:28).*

Suggested reading: Job 28:12-28

It was Hilary of Poitiers (c. 315-368) who once wrote, 'For He whom we can know only through his own utterances is a fitting witness concerning himself.'[1] No one apart from God himself can give us reliable information about God — who he is and what he does.

Apart from divine revelation, there can be no true and certain knowledge of God. This, of course, is aggravated by man's fall. Sin has darkened the understanding (Eph. 4:18; Rom. 3:11), but this is not Job's point here. He is, after all, pleading his righteousness. His point is not that he needs a Saviour; rather, what he needs is someone who will interpret for him the answers to his dilemma. Whilst sin does pose a massive problem in our capacity to understand the ways of God in this world, there is another problem: our *creatureliness*. We are so small! How can we possibly understand the wisdom of God?

Job's conclusion, then, is typical of what all the wisdom books say: we must *fear God* if we are ever to know any wisdom in this world! We must be ready to bow before the revelation that he has given of himself.

'Behold, the fear of the Lord, that is wisdom,
    and to turn away from evil is understanding'

(28:28).

It is exactly what the book of Proverbs says (Prov. 1:7; 9:10; cf. Ps. 111:10). And it provides the conclusion to the book of Ecclesiastes:

'The end of the matter; all has been heard. Fear God and keep his commandments, for this is the whole duty of man'

(Eccles. 12:13).

Reverence! That's the issue! Whether or not we hold God and his ways in awe — that is what really matters.

God is sovereign and Job must learn to bow before that sovereignty. In chapters 38 and 39, Job will be taught that in effect he knows nothing at all, in comparison with what God knows. How can he possibly expect to understand what God is doing in his life right now!

It is an issue of discipleship. There is a wisdom in a raindrop, Job is saying, that we cannot begin to understand (28:25-27). We must learn to exclaim: 'O the depths...' when we think of God and his providence in our lives. Job is reaffirming what he says in the very opening chapter:

'Naked I came from my mother's womb,
And naked shall I depart.
The LORD gave and the LORD has taken away;
Blessed be the name of the LORD'

(1:21).

But it is more than that. There is something here that Job could see only faintly, if at all. In a sense, his faith at this point is magnificent, for we baulk when far greater insights into the wisdom of God are given to us. The fear of God is a willingness to bow and say: 'Whatever the Lord does is right.'

There is every incentive for God's people to say that, because God's wisdom has been revealed to us in personal terms. God has revealed himself to us in his own Son, Jesus Christ. He *is* the wisdom of God (1 Cor. 1:24). He tells us, and shows us, things about God that otherwise we would never know, such as, God loves us with a love that is beyond our grasp; his covenant is certain; his word cannot be broken. We look to Jesus, and all that he has done on behalf of sinners, and we say that God is committed to our glorification. He will not rest until it is done. In some ways, our response of fear — the fear of God — is a response of a child who knows that his Father loves him even if he cannot fathom what his Father may be doing at any given moment. As Sinclair Ferguson has put it:

The fear of God defies our attempts at definition, because it is really another way of saying 'knowing God'. It is a heart-felt love for him because of who he is and what he has done; a sense of being in his majestic presence. It is a thrilling awareness that we have this greatest of all privileges, mingled with a realization that now the only thing that really matters is his opinion. To have the assurance of his smile is everything; to feel that he frowns on what we do is desolation. To fear God is to be sensitive to both his greatness and his graciousness. It is to know him and to love him wholeheartedly and unreservedly.[2]

Looking to Jesus Christ is the mirror by which we see the assurance of God's providential kindness to us even when we are in the dark. Job had glimpsed it in chapter 19 when he said that he knew that his Redeemer lived. It was his ultimate sanity in a situation which threatened it.

Wisdom will only come if we trust him this way. Our understanding will only flower as we walk in his ways. It will not come to us through bitterness, nor bickering, but through acquiescence and agreement, even when we cannot see it.

When the Mars Space Project was launched in 1999, scientists were confident of success. But the space probe burnt up in the Martian atmosphere. The reason? American and European scientists failed to synchronize to the same unit of measurement. Part of the software was reading in feet and inches, part in millimetres and centimetres. This failure to measure using the same system caused catastrophe. So it is when we attempt to measure providence by a different standard to that which God uses. The result will always be tragedy. As Job expresses so wonderfully here, we need to see things from the perspective the Lord himself provides.

Then, and only then, will there be peace in our hearts.

For your journal...

1. Think of ways that your responses to various situations (perhaps, a particular trial that you may be experiencing right now) fail to demonstrate a fear of God. What changes do you think might need to be made to better secure a greater reverence in your response to God's providences? Since this may well be the key to the entire book of Job we won't add any further questions!

Day 20
Longing for the former days

Job 29 – 31

*'God has cast me into the mire,
and I have become like dust and ashes.
I cry to you for help and you do not answer me;
I stand, and you only look at me'*
(Job 30:19-20).

Suggested reading: Job 30:1-15

These are Job's final words in this round of exchanges with his friends. After this, the strange figure of Elihu will appear, but Job will not respond to him. As a lawyer might do at the close of a trial, Job is presenting his final argument. It falls into three sections. It begins with a piece of nostalgia, a wistful longing for better and happier days that he had once known in his youth (chapter 29). Next comes a section in which he expresses just how 'low' he has become (chapter 30), his skin blackened and peeling, his body burning with fever (30:30). Finally, in chapter 31, Job has one more attempt to assert his innocence. The audacity of it takes our breath away — or is that because we, too, have joined forces with Job's friends in disbelieving his claims?

Let's take a moment to look at each one of these three parts of Job's closing argument.

Everyone's past becomes distorted. Some have unhappy childhoods that they wish to forget and recollections of it are sometimes 'adjusted' to ease the pain that memories bring. Some have wonderful experiences of growing up that become even idealized in the retelling. Job pictures halcyon days of his 'prime, when the friendship of God was upon my tent' (29:4). Each of us can perhaps imagine such a circumstance. My own thoughts drift to the seaside town of Aberystwyth in Wales when (in hindsight at least) everything seemed wonderful.

In a lengthy exposition of his earlier life, Job recalls the respect in which he was held, principally because of his godliness: 'I put on righteousness, and it clothed me; my justice was like a robe and a turban' (29:14). He 'lived like a king among his troops' (29:25). His every deed displayed the man of God that he was. Do you get the picture?

'When I went out to the gate of the city,
    when I prepared my seat in the square,
the young men saw me and withdrew,
    and the aged rose and stood;
the princes refrained from talking
    and laid their hand on their mouth;
the voice of the nobles was hushed,
    and their tongue stuck to the roof of their mouth.
When the ear heard, it called me blessed,
    and when the eye saw, it approved'

                                                    (29:7-11).

However idealized this picture may now be, the fact of the matter is that this is no longer Job's condition. No one respects him any more — worse than that — they are mocking him!

His words fall to the ground like lead. No one stands in awe of him any more.How low has Job sunk in his spirits?

> 'Terrors are turned upon me;
>> my honour is pursued as by the wind,
> and my prosperity has passed away like a cloud'
>
> (30:15).

Job's life is 'ebbing away' (30:16, NIV). God has fixed a noose around him and thrown him into the mud (30:18-19). He is tossed about by a storm (v. 22), and death seems imminent (v. 23). His prayers are unanswered (v. 20). His every hope has been dashed (v. 25). 'My inward parts are in turmoil and never still,' he cries (v. 27). With no relief from medication or friend, his every plea goes unheeded. He sings the blues:

> 'My lyre is turned to mourning,
>> and my pipe to the voice of those who weep'
>
> (v. 31).

This is about as sad a piece of writing as there is to be found anywhere in literature. Nothing has surpassed its melancholy. It is impossible to read it and not feel the deepest sympathy for Job. There are faint echoes to which some of us can relate, but few of God's children have walked these dark passages. But those who have will find here a note that induces hope: hope that springs from the knowledge that someone else has been here, too; hope that insists that we are not, after all, alone in our suffering.

From such blackened pages as these there springs forth a faint ray of light. For through such darkness as this our Saviour passed. What depth of grief he felt when he uttered his cry of forsakenness on the cross, it is impossible to tell; but, that he passed through a sense of utter abandonment — by man *and* God — is certain.

> O Cross, that liftest up my head,
> I dare not ask to fly from thee;
> I lay in dust life's glory dead,
> And from the ground there blossoms red
> Life that shall endless be.
>
> George Matheson (1842-1906)

Job may feel grief-stricken and abandoned, but he has a little more breath in him to give one final cry of innocence. In a series of statements that begin with 'if' he makes plain that *if* he has sinned in some way punishment is what he deserves. This is the moral nature of the universe that has maintained Job's sanity all along. He dare not give up on it now or all is indeed 'vanity', as the writer of Ecclesiastes suggests some thirty or so times. No, Job will not go down that path or else all hope is gone. He will insist upon his argument, even if God will not hear him. But he will have one more attempt to get a hearing:

> 'Oh, that I had one to hear me!
>   (Here is my signature! Let the Almighty answer me!)
> Oh, that I had the indictment written by my adversary!'
>
> (31:35).

The truth is, God does hear him! And God will write down his verdict as Job has asked (Job's 'adversary' here is not Satan [the Hebrew is different from 1:6], but God). The book of Job, inspired by the Holy Spirit and preserved for us to read and study, contains God's agreement with Job's assessment. Job has spoken out of turn, he has impugned God in a way that will earn him a rebuke; but Job is not suffering because of his sin, as his friends have suggested.

To that extent, Job is right. But God does not tell him so as yet. There is more silence from heaven to endure and more advice from someone who thinks he understands the situation.

Can you be patient and wait for God?

Wait for the LORD;
   be strong, and let your heart take courage;
wait for the LORD!

(Ps. 27:14).

For your journal...

1. What do you think about Christians who are melancholic, or even depressed? How sympathetic are you? When Job's 'lyre' is 'turned to mourning', do you have the urge to say to him, 'Cheer up!'?

2. Many of the psalms reflect the sombre, even despondent mood of these closing chapters in Job. Since the church has sung these psalms in public worship (at least, this was the case until recently even if only a few churches continue to do so), what does this have to say to us about the narrow focus of so much of contemporary Christianity? Does the lack of emphasis upon a well-rounded emotional response to God and his ways distort our understanding of the nature of the Christian life, or not?

Day 21
Enter Elihu

Job 32

'And shall I wait, because they do not speak,
because they stand there, and answer no more?
I also will answer with my share;
I also will declare my opinion'
(Job 32:16-17).

Suggested reading: Job 32:1-12

The three friends have been reduced to silence; they are all 'talked out'. They have failed in their attempt to get Job to say, 'This is all my fault!' They have also failed as instruments of Satan in getting Job to curse God. Remember, this had been Satan's point from the beginning — that if God were to remove from Job all his material comforts, he would 'curse you to your face' (1:11). But so far at least, Job has come short of that.

Suddenly, we learn that there is a fourth counsellor present — Elihu. He is evidently younger than the other three counsellors (32:6), and this accounts for the fact that he has waited until now to say something. Up to this point, he has been silent, but now he is 'bursting' to speak (v. 19).

He has evidently been there in the wings, listening, taking everything in. He has heard Job's shrieks of innocence. He has listened as Job has questioned the integrity of God and the justice of providence. Patience or respect has held him back, but the three friends have fallen silent and an opportunity presents itself for him to say something.

Elihu explodes with anger! Anger, both at the three inept friends, and also with Job. If we think the three friends are long-winded, they are the epitome of brevity in comparison with rambling Elihu! He will take six chapters (165 verses) to make his point.

Three times (four in the Hebrew text) we are told that he 'burned with anger' (32:2 [twice in Hebrew], 3, 5). His anger at the three counsellors is understandable (v. 3). Their unrelenting and unflinching message has been difficult to accept. Suffering is always the result of God's punishment on some sin or other, they have insisted. They have sung this song of 'instant retribution with no exceptions' to death. 'You get what you deserve; no more, no less,' they have pontificated. There is nothing more they can say. And Elihu's indignation is appropriate. They have been wrong theologically and pastorally. Their manner of approach and their message has shown little understanding or compassion. We, too, are irritated by their monotony and heartlessness.

But why is he angry with Job? Because he believes Job was 'justifying himself rather than God' (v. 2). Job has gone too far in his cries of innocence. He has protested too much and too often for Elihu's liking. Enough is enough!

Elihu is right, of course. There is only one who has lived in this world who is without sin — Jesus Christ. He alone could ask with unqualified conviction, 'Which one of you convicts me of sin?' (John 8:46). So assured has Job been of his faultlessness that he speaks with a confidence that is breathtaking. He has entered into an oath in his own defence, signed it and is prepared to defend it vigorously. 'Surely I would carry it on my shoulder; I would bind it on me as a crown' (Job 31:36). He has challenged his accuser to prove he is in error, whoever that accuser may be, his friends (collectively); or perhaps God himself! Either way, Job is ready to go to court and defend himself. Who of us would ever have such confidence? Or is it arrogance?

Before we shake our heads and say, 'Job! How can you say that?' we must recall yet again that God has already informed us in the prologue of Job's 'innocence'. However tempting it is to join Job's critics, we cannot deny that Job has a defensible case. We dare not now capitulate at this late stage and side with the counsellors after all and say, 'I have this sneaking suspicion that there just might be some secret sin somewhere that has not been confessed.' That would be to unravel the entire argument that has been carefully defended. No, Job's suffering has nothing to do with his past.

However, while all that is true of Job *before* the trial, it has become woefully apparent that Job has overstepped the mark *since* the onset of the trial. There were those sublime moments initially when Job responded with such poise and grace: 'Naked I came from my mother's womb, and naked shall I return. The LORD gave, and the LORD has taken away; blessed be the name of the LORD' (1:21), we heard him say. All of us want to be able to respond just like that. But since then, the poise has disappeared. The grace has been clouded.

Job has given us more than a little cause for discomfort as he has sought to defend himself.

He has by now given more than sufficient reason to say, 'Job, you have said too much.' He has questioned the integrity of

God. He has called into question God's faithfulness to his covenant children. He has made God out to be his enemy. He no longer has any confidence that God will give him a fair hearing in court.

All of this has ignited Elihu's ire. Job has gone too far! God's honour now needs defending and Elihu is going to do it. What does Elihu say?

The six chapters that contain Elihu's four speeches (32-37) are a summary of Elihu's contribution to the 'problem' of Job's suffering. Many commentators are dismissive of his contribution, for two principal reasons. In the first place, Elihu is merely reflecting the same prejudices and simplistic analysis as the three friends. In the second place, when God addresses the contributions of the friends at the close of the book, he says nothing at all about Elihu. Whilst the three friends are roundly criticized by God, Elihu gets away without so much as a mention. This, some suggest, is a silence that speaks volumes. By ignoring his contribution, God does the most devastating thing possible — he condemns it to oblivion.

There are, however, some cogent responses to both of these objections. It is true that Elihu descends into the same 'instant retribution' theology that has characterized so much of the earlier speeches of Bildad, Eliphaz and Zophar. There are times when what Elihu says sounds little different to that of the 'righteousness is always rewarded, sin is always punished' view expressed at length already by Job's three friends. However, it is also true that Elihu has some new and insightful elements in his speeches that add significantly to the issue of Job's suffering. We will take a look at these positive elements tomorrow when we shall have another cause to examine Elihu's contributions.

Elihu takes a chapter and a half to get to the point! Not until 33:12 does he begin his argument. He has introduced himself with deference and not a little verbosity, and here is his contribution that will make sense of it all: Job's claim to sinlessness is wrong! This is how he puts it:

> 'Surely you have spoken in my ears,
>   and I have heard the sound of your words.
> You say, "I am pure, without transgression;
>   I am clean, and there is no iniquity in me..."
> Behold, in this you are not right. I will answer you,
>   for God is greater than man'
>
> (33:8-9, 12).

But, had Job ever said such a thing? Had Job ever really claimed sinlessness? Earlier, Eliphaz had heard Job utter the same claim (15:14-16), but Job had never actually said this. He had acknowledged his sinfulness on more than one occasion (7:21; 13:26). At the risk of sounding as repetitive as these counsellors, what Job had insisted upon was the con-nection between his suffering and *one particular sin*. Job could not see it.

Some have seen Elihu's contribution as definitive. They have discerned the voice of God in his words. Calvin, for example, seems to rest his entire interpretation of Job on these words of Elihu. But it is hard not to see a grievous error in his opening words, an error that makes whatever else he will say suspect and flawed. Already, he has taken and twisted Job's words to mean something else. And in counselling, failure *to hear* is a grievous failure indeed!

Jesus never twists our words to mean something else. Never! We will never have cause to say to him, 'But, I never said that!' or 'That's not what I meant.' Isn't that all the reassurance we need to run to him and pour out our woes? Then do it!

For your journal...

1. To what extent is Elihu correct in his assessment that Job has been 'justifying himself rather than God' (32:2)? In what ways can this be true if we agree with Job's assertion of innocence?

2. Do you think that Elihu is unfair in asserting that Job had claimed to be free from sin? What does this say about the way we listen to others who find themselves in trouble? Do we sometimes make unfair assessments of other people's positions?

Day 22
Finding a purpose in suffering

Job 33 – 37

'Man is also rebuked with pain on his bed
and with continual strife in his bones...
Behold, God does all these things,
twice, three times, with a man,
to bring back his soul from the pit...'
(Job 33:19, 29-30).

Suggested reading: Job 33:1-14

Elihu paints an elaborate picture, which amounts to the fact that however much trouble we receive, it does not match up to what we deserve when we take into consideration our fallen nature. In a graphic portrayal of human suffering, Elihu says:

'Man is also rebuked with pain on his bed
    and with continual strife in his bones,
so that his life loathes bread,
    and his appetite the choicest food.
His flesh is so wasted away that it cannot be seen,
    and his bones that were not seen stick out.
His soul draws near the pit,
    and his life to those who bring death'

(33:19-22).

Then Elihu imagines that a 'mediator' will plead for him, and he is spared from 'going down to the pit' so that as a consequence:

> "'Let his flesh become fresh with youth;
>   let him return to the days of his youthful vigour";
> then man prays to God, and he accepts him;
>   he sees his face with a shout of joy,
> and he restores to man his righteousness.
>   He sings before men and says:
> "I sinned and perverted what was right,
>   and it was not repaid to me.
> He has redeemed my soul from going down into the pit,
>   and my life shall look upon the light."
> Behold, God does all these things,
>   twice, three times, with a man,
> to bring back his soul from the pit,
>   that he may be lighted with the light of life'
>
> (33:25-30).

Elihu's point is that suffering can teach us something about ourselves. Job may not have been punished for some past sin, but the suffering has disclosed how far he is capable of falling. Job's life may have been blameless before the trial; but the events of these last days have shown just how his own heart can be led into ways that otherwise he might have thought impossible. Suffering can show us the sinfulness of our hearts.

Suffering can lead us to appreciate God's love in new ways.

We are to treasure every providence that shows us what we are capable of doing when left to our own devices. What sin could we fall into when God withdraws his hand? How far down can we slide into the abyss if God steps back just a little? When it is just ourselves and Satan, what are we capable of saying? Of thinking? Of doing? Job has begun to discover the sinfulness of his heart when trial strikes and he will confess before too long, 'Therefore I despise myself and repent in dust and ashes' (42:6).

Every glimpse of innate depravity is to be welcomed. Such providences are God's way of saying to us: 'This is what you really are without my grace. Everything that you now are, you are because of me.' Elihu has caught a glimpse of a truth that we need to hold dear: that at our very best, we are sinners saved by grace alone. We will never get beyond that. Even in paradise, we shall bear the collective memory of the work of the Saviour that was needed to wash and cleanse us from the pollution of sin.

What Elihu is trying to grasp, and he is doing so only faintly, is the truth that is brought out in John Newton's poem, 'Prayer Answered by Crosses'. Here is a Christian eager to grow in grace and asking God for greater holiness and consecration. What is God's answer? Crosses! Pain! Suffering!

> I asked the Lord that I might grow
> In faith, and love, and every grace;
> Might more of his salvation know,
> And seek more earnestly his face.
>
> I thought that in some favoured hour
> At once he'd answer my request;
> And, by his love's constraining power,
> Subdue my sins, and give me rest.

Instead of this, he made me feel
The hidden evils of my heart,
And let the angry powers of hell
Assault my soul in every part.

'Lord, why is this?' I trembling cried,
'Wilt thou pursue thy worm to death?'
'Tis in this way,' the Lord replied,
'I answer prayer for grace and faith.'

'These inward trials I employ
From self and pride to set thee free,
And break thy schemes of earthly joy,
That thou may'st seek thy all in me!'

That is what I believe Elihu is trying to say. Sometimes God
will abandon us to our own devices and the onslaughts of the
devil in order to make us appreciate all the more his tender
care and mercy to us. Suffering can teach us the true nature
of our hearts and can urge us to trust in the sovereign care of
a God who is 'our Father in heaven'. It can also do something
else. It can fill our minds with questions to which there are no
easily discernible answers. Suffering can paint the canvas of a
providence that is beyond our ability to fathom. It can exalt
the majesty of God.

It is one thing to appreciate God's mercy to us as sinners; it
is another to appreciate his greatness because we are his creatures. Elihu makes this very point in the fourth and final speech:

'Behold, God is great, and we know him not;
    the number of his years is unsearchable'

(36:26).

'God thunders wondrously with his voice;
> he does great things that we cannot comprehend'
>> (37:5).

God is great! And not a little of the implication of God's majesty is the fact that his ways can never be understood by man. His ways are not our ways; his thoughts are not our thoughts (cf. Isa. 55:8). There is a chasm of infinite width that divides God's mind from ours. We cannot ever expect to discern what he is doing unless he tells us. Sometimes, what he does looks so baffling and so strange, that all we can do is wonder! It should cause us to tremble a little.

This is part of the lesson that Paul learned with his 'thorn in the flesh'. This, too, was 'a messenger of Satan' just as Job's suffering had been (though Job was unaware of it; cf. 2 Cor. 12:7). Just as it had been for Job, the suffering for Paul was difficult to accept; three times he asked for its removal. Acquiescence and passivity is not implicit in the Christian view of sainthood. It is noteworthy and moving that even our Saviour sought for the removal of the cup in the Garden of Gethsemane. His holiness is evidenced, not in the absence of struggle, but in the submission he eventually offered. Job, too, has been struggling and not without lapse in his case. Yet, the struggle has taught him something that he needs to learn: that sainthood involves submission to the will of God, *even when that will is beyond our understanding.*

Pain can teach us submission in a way that nothing else can. It can drive us to God for help in a way that nothing else does. Paul records having seen 'visions and revelations' which he was not permitted to relate (2 Cor. 12:1, 4). To ensure that Paul was kept from pride, God allowed a thorn in the flesh to torment him. God permitted Satan to harass him. Amongst the most mysterious and challenging issues in life is not the fact that Satan harasses us — that is understandable. The problem is that God permits it. It is part of his will that Satan sift us as wheat (Luke 22:31-32). Satan cannot do it of his own volition alone. He cannot come straight from hell. He must first appear before God and be given his assignment (Job 1:12; 2:6). This challenges everything we think we know about God. God sent Satan to keep Paul from becoming 'conceited' (2 Cor. 12:7, NIV). But, the staggering thing is that God did not take the trial away. Instead, Paul had to learn to endure it; he had to adopt the servant attitude, which says, 'God knows what he is doing. He is able to help me no matter what the trouble may be. His grace will be sufficient.'

God knows what he is doing! In the end Job must come to confess this. He must learn that God is not obligated to answer his demands and give an explanation that will satisfy him. Job must learn to lay his hand on his mouth and acknowledge that it is not important that he understands; it is important only that God does.

That is where Job will be brought once Elihu has stopped speaking.

Are you ready for God to humble you *that much*? Are you prepared to say *nothing* in your defence? Are you ready to let God have his way even if every fibre of your being wants to scream?

Have thine own way, Lord! Have thine own way!
 Thou art the potter, I am the clay.
Mould me and make me after thy will,
 while I am waiting, yielded and still.
      Adelaide A. Pollard (1862-1934)

For your journal...

1. What have you learned through suffering that you do not think could have been learned in any other way? Write them down in your journal carefully, asking yourself the question, 'Have I yielded myself to these troubles in the sense that Paul could say, "I have learned in whatever situation I am to be content"?' (Phil. 4:11).

2. What does the word 'submission' mean for you? What shape would it take in your life? What things would be different?

Day 23
The voice of God

Job 38

'Then the Lord answered Job out of the whirlwind and said:
"Who is this that darkens counsel
by words without knowledge?"'
(Job 38:1-2).

Suggested reading: Job 38:1-15

Asaph, the Jerusalem choir-director, found himself in a similar position to Job. Wickedness was rewarded and godliness punished; or so it seemed. Life did not make a great deal of sense. 'But when I thought how to understand this, it seemed to me a wearisome task,' he confessed (Ps. 73:16). Trying to make sense of God's ways in this world gave him a headache!

Job is aching, too. He has been questioning God; yes, questioning *God!* And it has got him nowhere. His friends have condemned him. Even Elihu, whose contribution seemed to promise an answer, has now fallen silent.

Perhaps it is the silence that hurts most. Why hasn't *God* said something? Thirty-seven chapters have gone by and God has said *nothing!* Of course, he has spoken to Satan in the opening prologue; but Job knew nothing about that. As far as Job is concerned, God does not seem to care about his plight.

It is one of those things the psalmist loved to think about: that *God cares* (Ps. 8:4; 95:7; 144:3). But Job has lost sight of this. Pain has cast shadows over the landscape such that its details can no longer be discerned.

Chapter 38 brings us, at last, to what looks like the answer we have been looking for. God is about to speak to Job. The silence is broken. The resolution of Job's enquiries about life and tragedy are about to be explained: 'Then the LORD answered Job...' (38:1). God has not made any sense to Job so far, but all that is about to change. Light is going to be shed on the subject and answers are going to be given.

If Job will be patient for just a minute or two longer...

But, wait! What is this? 'Then the LORD answered Job *out of the whirlwind...*' A whirlwind?

After this agonizing silence you might expect God to come to Job as a shepherd might to a poor, lost lamb. You might expect him to pick up Job in his arms and whisper words of love and reassurance in his ear.

You might expect God to behave as a father might on seeing one of his children fallen and crying. The child's face is all crumpled up with pain and frustration, longing for the warmth of a familiar embrace. You might expect God to pick up Job as a nursing mother might, saying, 'There, there, there ... everything is going to be all right.'

But a storm? Twice we are told that God speaks to Job out of a whirlwind (38:1; 40:6). Why?

God appears this way at Mount Sinai, for example. 'Mount Sinai was covered with smoke ... the smoke billowed up from it like smoke from a furnace, the whole mountain trembled violently...' (Exod. 19:18, NIV; cf. Heb. 12:18-21). Something similar happens in the opening chapter of Ezekiel, when God manifests himself in a 'stormy wind ... a great cloud, with brightness around it, and fire flashing forth continually, and in the midst of the fire, as it were gleaming metal' (Ezek. 1:4).

Is this some theatrical 'fireworks' display intended to introduce an element of drama? No! It is the Bible's way of telling us what God is really like! There is something about him that intimidates! Yes, *intimidates!*

That this is not all there is to God is equally important to stress; God loves his children with a love that is indescribably strong and passionate. But he is also holy. And for now, this is what he wants Job to understand.

In the first of God's speeches to Job (38:1 – 39:30), he appears to be saying two things of equal and inseparable importance. One has to do with God himself; the other concerns Job.

There was a cry at the heart of the Reformation, particularly in Luther's assessment of the contribution of the humanist, Erasmus: 'Your God is too small.' Downsizing God has been a fashionable trend in theology throughout this past century, both in liberal and evangelical assessments of who God is. The most recent controversy of our times has to do with God's knowledge of the future, some suggesting that the future is 'open' rather than determined. God-shrinkers abound!

'Dress for action like a man,' God says (38:3). The verb employed may well come from a Hebrew word for wrestling. Job has been asking for a fight! Now, he is about to get one. It is not a fight about physical strength, of course, but a fight about wisdom. The stage is set: God will ask the questions, and Job will answer (38:3). Already, we get the impression that this is not a contest between equals. The scales seem to be weighted against Job from the start!

What is the first question? 'Where were you when I laid the foundation of the earth?' (38:4).

It is a devastating question that has Job reeling in response. 'That's not fair!' we almost hear Job saying. Ask me something that I can answer!

But God hasn't finished! He has only just begun! There are more questions to follow, many more, and we will have to consider these tomorrow. For now, it is important to ask why God begins like this. Even though we may guess at the answer, it is right to assume that Job was floored by this approach. I am certain his mind was reeling as God spoke to him. Job was probably shocked, hurt, and perhaps even angry. For now he says nothing, but the encounter has shaken him to the core. He had not expected this at all.

When God behaves in unexpected ways, it shakes our entire belief-system. God's silence and then his initial response have both challenged Job's expectations. It suggests that his view of God had been in error to some degree.

In just the same way we can find ourselves shocked by Jesus' responses: when Jairus tells Jesus that his daughter had just died and urgently requests his presence that she may be healed, Jesus delays a visit by healing a woman with a haemorrhage (Matt. 9:18-26). When Jesus is asked by his mother about the wine problem at the wedding in Cana, he replies (in a manner that appears terse), 'Woman, what does this have to do with me? My hour has not yet come' (John 2:4). When a rich young man asks him about the way to inherit eternal life, Jesus replies by referring him to the Ten Commandments and then allows him to walk away (Mark 10:17-31).

Our view of God is too small. That is the problem.
And this leads us into trouble.

Job's *theology* is wrong. His view of God is wrong. Before he can begin to address the problem of pain, he must first address another problem — a shrunken God who is there to be commanded. And God will have none of it!

Is that the problem you face — a shrunken God? Have you reduced his wisdom? His power? His holiness? His justice? His goodness? His truth?

For your journal...

1. If you had been writing the story of Job, and in the thirty-eighth chapter you are finally introducing the words of God, what do you think they might be? Imagine some possible scenarios and compare them to the actual way God's words are introduced.

2. Is God meant to intimidate us as Christians? Does this have any place at all in your theology?

Day 24
Questions, questions and more questions!

Job 38 - 39

'Have you comprehended the expanse of the earth?
Declare, if you know all this'
(Job 38:18).

Suggested reading Job 39:1-8

God has answered Job's request for a hearing with a battery of questions! He had begun with a teaser: 'Where were you when I laid the foundation of the earth?' (38:4). This had been impossible for Job to answer, but it was only the first in a series of questions. Questions like:

'Who determined its measurements — surely you know!
Or who stretched the line upon it?'

(38:5).

And *more* questions!

'Have you commanded the morning since your days began,
and caused the dawn to know its place,

that it might take hold of the skirts of the earth,
    and the wicked be shaken out of it?'

(38:12-13).

And *more* questions!

'Have you comprehended the expanse of the earth?
    Declare, if you know all this'

(38:18).

And *more* questions!

'Can you bind the chains of the Pleiades
    or loose the cords of Orion?
Can you lead forth the Mazzaroth in their season,
    or can you guide the Bear with its children?
Do you know the ordinances of the heavens?
Can you establish their rule on the earth?'

(38:31-33).

And *more* questions!

'Do you give the horse his might?
    Do you clothe his neck with a mane?'

(39:19).

And *more* questions!

'Is it by your understanding that the hawk soars
    and spreads his wings towards the south?
Is it at your command that the eagle mounts up
    and makes his nest on high?'

(39:26-27).

In these two chapters (38 and 39), there are almost fifty questions put to Job, none of which he can answer! Only God is able to answer them. They are questions about the earth, the sea, constellations, the weather, light and darkness, animals and birds.

The point? To underline what Scripture will testify that God is great (Deut. 7:21; Neh. 4:14; Ps. 48:1; 86:10; 95:3; 145:3; Dan. 9:4). He is greater than we can grasp. Look at what he knows in comparison with what we know, and you get the point, it seems to be saying. He understands things so much better than we ever can. God dwells in unapproachable light (Ps. 97:2; 1 Tim. 6:16). He is so far above us that we cannot possibly understand him or his ways. Do not be surprised that providence is beyond your grasp, that you cannot unravel it: God *himself* is beyond your grasp. What we understand of God, we understand because he has, to use Calvin's phrase, accommodated himself to our capacity. He has used 'baby-talk' to make himself known. He has used metaphor and simile to give 'substance' to his form. Thus, we speak of him as having eyes, and ears, and hands, knowing all along that he has none of these things (e.g. Exod. 33:11; 1 Sam. 5:11; Neh. 1:6; Isa. 53:1).

William Henry Green has captured the point well:

> It might upon the first superficial view of the case appear as though the discourse of the LORD had no particular relevance to the circumstances in which it was uttered. And the question might arise what these appeals to the magnificence of the works of God in nature have to do with the solution of the enigma to which this book is devoted. How do they contribute to the explanation of the mystery that is involved in the sufferings of good men?

The fact is, this discourse is not directed to an eluci-
dation of that mystery at all. It is not the design of God
to offer a vindication of his dealings with men in general,
or a justification of his providence towards Job. He has
no intention of placing himself at the bar of his creatures and elevating them into judges of his conduct. He
is not amenable to them and he does not recognize their
right to be censors of him and of his ways.[1]

That is it exactly! God is not about to answer Job's
questions! He will ask questions of his own. Job must appreciate
that God is so great, so beyond his grasp, that he cannot
possibly fathom the divine mind. To expect otherwise is to
shrink God down to our size. And God will not allow us to do
that! 'Let God be God!' was the watch-cry of the Reformation.

There is a parallel issue that we must consider. Not only is
God enlarging his own greatness in Job's eyes, he is also simul-
taneously shrinking Job's estimation of himself. If Job's God is
too small, Job's estimation of himself is too great. He has
allowed himself to think that he deserves an answer from God.
For Job, it is a matter of his rights. God is obligated to explain
himself to him. Job has set himself as judge and entered a verdict. God's providence is not fair!

There is a mystery to the divine being. Herman Bavinck
begins his book, *The Doctrine of God,* with the sentence:
'Mystery is the vital element of dogmatics.'[2] There has to be
an appreciation of what the medieval church rendered: *finitum
non capax infiniti* — the finite cannot comprehend the infinite. God is incomprehensible to us — not that he cannot be
understood at all, but that he cannot be understood fully. His
holiness renders our grasp of the Almighty God severely

limited. This is not so much a problem of sin, though sin has seriously affected our ability to understand anything that is spiritual. The problem is one of finitude: we are *too small* to understand the ways of God.

In the presence of high mountain glaciers, where ice and snow reside year-round, God asks:

'Have you entered the storehouses of the snow,
  or have you seen the storehouses of the hail'

(38:22).

No, he had not. There are places in this earth that few can ever ascend to.

'Can you lift up your voice to the clouds,
  that a flood of waters may cover you?...
Who can number the clouds by wisdom?
  Or who can tilt the waterskins of the heavens?'

(38:34, 37).

No man can order the clouds to move an inch to the left or to the right. They operate by powers that are beyond our ability to control. Until Job realizes how *small* he is, he is not at the point where God wants him to be.

What the book of Job does here to humble Job's pride, the Bible does elsewhere in order to encourage the people of God! Reminding us of God's power can, on the one hand, prick the balloon of pride; on the other hand, it can energize flagging faith.

When Isaiah wanted to encourage flagging faith in the face of oppression and exile, he utters these words:

'He sits enthroned above the circle of the earth,
    and its people are like grasshoppers.
He stretches out the heavens like a canopy,
    and spreads them out like a tent to live in...
"To whom will you compare me?
    Or who is my equal?" says the Holy One.
Lift your eyes and look to the heavens:
    Who created all these?
He who brings out the starry host one by one,
    and calls them each by name'

(Isa. 40:22, 25-26, NIV).

His point? Think about how great the world really is! And yet, everything in it dwarfs in comparison to the greatness of God. The world is his footstool, and he sits secure above it. Think of the stars! Nothing can make you feel your smallness more than gazing at the stars. In our galaxy alone, there is thought to be something in the region of 100,000 million stars. And there are some estimated 100,000 million galaxies. Distances boggle the mind when the light from the clearest star (Polaris, or North Star) takes 350 years to get here travelling at 186,000 miles per second! The light from that star began its journey to us just after the Westminster Assembly sat in Westminster, London, in the 1640s!

We really are small! And unless we grasp it, our usefulness is seriously curtailed.

The point will reach its culmination later on, when Job lays his hand over his mouth (40:4). Job has been *silenced*. Like a wild horse, he has been broken. Pain has made him like a servant.

We have no usefulness until we reach that point of quiescence. Until our souls are still, God holds us at bay. It is a hard lesson — the hardest lesson of all!

Writing of her time in the Republic of Congo [Zaire] when she had been abducted and raped, Helen Roseveare came to realize this truth in the most painful of ways:

On that dreadful night [29 October 1964], beaten and bruised, terrified and tormented, unutterably alone, I had felt at last that even God had failed me. Surely He could have stepped in earlier, surely things need not have gone that far. I had reached what seemed to me the ultimate depth of despairing nothingness. Yet even as my heart had cried out against God for His failure and my mental anguish taunted me to doubt His very existence, another reasoning had made itself felt.

'You asked Me, when you were first converted, for the privilege of being a missionary. This is it: don't you want it?'

Events had moved so fast: everything seemed to happen at once. Pain and cruelty and humiliation had continued in an ever-growing crescendo, yet with it, a strange peace and deep consciousness that God was in charge and knew what He was doing. Odd thoughts and phrases and impulses broke through, and later on were woven together to show the inner meaning of the events of that night, but it had not been orderly, in a way one could set down on paper or explain in a lecture.

'These are not your sufferings: they are Mine. All I ask of you is the loan of your body.'[3]

Nothing can make the point clearer than that. Jesus wants us to be his servants, and that may mean being bruised and beaten in the process. He was beaten and bruised for us, and sometimes he asks us to follow in those steps too. We may not know why; all we may know is that God has asked us to take it.

Are we ready for this?

For your journal...

1. What does it mean when the Bible says, 'God is great' (Job 36:26; 1 Chron. 16:25; Ps. 35:27; 40:16; 48:1; 70:4; 77:13; 96:4; 145:3)? How does the answer to this affect the nature of our discipleship? Can you suggest ways in which we can demonstrate the greatness of God *in our responses to life situations?*

Day 25
Dungeons and dragons

Job 40

'Behold, Behemoth,
which I made as I made you…'
(Job 40:15).

Suggested reading: Job 40:15-24

Did you ever ask yourself why God made the hippopotamus? Strange question? Yes! Especially for Job, in the situation he was in.

Imagine it! Job is dying; he has suffered incalculable loss and pain. And he is asked: 'Did you ever think about the hippopotamus?' You have to admit, this is a little strange. And yet, this is what apparently happens. It makes no sense. It leaves us baffled for a moment, even resentful that God seems to toy with Job, unsympathetic to his condition. It sounds like mockery.

Actually, the creature God alludes to in chapter 40 is not really a hippopotamus at all, but something called 'the Behemoth'. 'Behold, Behemoth, which I made…' (v. 15). Modern interpretations of this creature have tried to identify it with the hippo, but not with any great enthusiasm. Others have declared their allegiance to the rhinoceros. Older interpreters preferred to think that what God was talking about here was an elephant. The truth is, the description does not fit any of these creatures with ease. There is something 'fantastic' about its description. Some have even attempted to identify it with a prehistoric creature, one of the dinosaurs that roamed the earth prior to the Flood.

Nor is this all. The next chapter opens with a description of something called 'Leviathan' (41:1). Again, some modern interpreters think this is a crocodile, whilst older ones prefer to think of it as a whale. It is certainly a creature of the water, but when you read its description you will find yourself scratching your head and saying, 'This is not like anything I've ever seen!'

Elephant, rhinoceros, or hippopotamus; whale, or crocodile, it does not really matter; all are creatures that look a little odd. You might be forgiven for thinking that they resemble something a committee might have come up with! Everything about them seems out of proportion, cartoon-like exaggerations of mysterious creatures hard to describe without raising a wry smile.

What is more puzzling is not so much the identity of Behemoth or Leviathan, but that forty-four verses should be devoted to them at this point in the story.

Think about it: Job is at his wit's end, and finally God has spoken! He has come with a series of about fifty questions on the nature and origin of the universe. Job has responded to this 'ordeal' — for that is what it was, a trial of wisdom — by submitting to his divine opponent the response of ignorance. He simply did not know the answer to any of God's questions. Job has to confess to his limitations as a finite human being. He cannot possibly be expected to understand God's providence any more than he can understand the complexity of the origin and behaviour of the universe in which he lives.

But there is more to Job's dilemma. He has not only been unreasonable in his demands, asking for answers that he could not possibly have understood even if they had been given him, Job has also been sinful in his criticisms of the Almighty. He has already lost the first round of this battle, saying: 'I lay my hand on my mouth... I will proceed no further' (40:4-5).

'Best of three...' we almost hear Job saying! And so he must now prepare for another round:

'Dress for action like a man;
  I will question you, and you
    make it known to me'

(40:7).

In his book *A Grief Observed*, C. S. Lewis noted that we can sometimes ask questions which God finds unanswerable! Questions like: How many hours are there in a mile? 'Probably half the questions we ask — half our great theological and metaphysical problems — are like that.'[1]

But Job's problem had extended further than merely asking silly questions. Job had been angry with God. In being angry, he had entered into judgement of God and his ways. God had been placed 'in the dock'. Job had, in effect, set himself *above* God. He had committed man's most prevalent sin: making himself a god. As Eden-like as this is, Job must now face a deeper reality than his ignorance. He must face up to the *sinfulness* of his response. If Job had been morally 'blameless' *before* the trial, he had not been *during* it.

In what must be one of the most startling passages in this extraordinary book, God throws down the gauntlet. If Job really does/can discern right and wrong, then let him extend his fury and judge accordingly.

'Have you an arm like God,
  and can you thunder with a voice like his?
Adorn yourself with majesty and dignity;
  clothe yourself with glory and splendour.
Pour out the overflowings of your anger,
  and look on everyone who is proud and abase him.
Look on everyone who is proud and bring him low
  and tread down the wicked where they stand.
Hide them all in the dust together;
  bind their faces in the world below.
Then will I also acknowledge to you
  that your own right hand can save you'

                                              (40:9-14).

If Job can do this, God will worship at Job's feet! Job will be acknowledged as divine.

It is breathtaking, isn't it? Job has been reducing God, and what God is doing is bringing Job down to size.

This *reduction* of God in our minds has been going on since Adam's time. We think we *know* better than God does. Not only that we know better, but that this gives us the moral edge. We *are* better than God! Somehow, in this whole business of asking moral and theological questions, we assume that our opinion is the right one. We do it all the time, putting God in the dock along with everyone and everything else. We make ourselves God, by making our moral sense the judge of everything.

It is not so much our ignorance as our impiety that offends.

Already, we get the impression that Job is being humbled. And humility, as Jesus taught his disciples, is the key to greatness. Growing up involves growing down, becoming like children (Matt. 18:1-6).

Be prepared for humbling experiences in your relationship with God!

For your journal...

1. How did you respond when you discovered that God would ask Job about Behemoth and Leviathan? Why is it that we react negatively to this?

2. How can the study of creation help us take pleasure in God? (Jonathan Edwards made a study of bass, leaning over a boat in a lake!)

Day 26
The faint glimmer
of comprehension

Job 41

'Can you draw out Leviathan with a fishhook
or press down his tongue with a cord?'
(Job 41:1).

Suggested reading: Job 41:1-11

Don't you think Job might have been saying to himself: 'This is like a nightmare! Here I am, about to die, and God is asking me about scary animals! He cannot be serious!' Yes, he is!

But why does God ask about *Behemoth* and *Leviathan?* And what are they exactly? And what in the world has this to do with Job's problem?

Behemoth! We have already noted such suggestions as the elephant, or the rhinoceros, or even the hippopotamus. But the description that follows, especially of 'his tail stiff like a cedar' (40:17), does not fit any of these creatures. Henry M. Morris has made a convincing case that Behemoth represents a dinosaur, a creature now extinct but not so in Job's time.[1]

The same applies to Leviathan. This creature is capable of breathing out fire!

'His sneezings flash forth light,
   and his eyes are like the eyelids of the dawn.
Out of his mouth go flaming torches;
   sparks of fire leap forth'

(41:18-19).

A fire-breathing dragon![2] Interesting as this is, there is another interpretation that calls for our attention. The book of Job has already used the word 'Leviathan' in chapter 3. There, it seems to function as a synonym for 'death' (3:8). Jewish interpreters have been almost unanimous in their interpretation of both Leviathan and Behemoth as symbolic of all that is evil. An entire mythology of evil grew using these creatures to depict it. Nor is this difficult for us to imagine. Those who love the writings of C. S. Lewis or J. R. R. Tolkien are familiar with the genre of mythological creatures depicting forces of good and evil, whether it be *The Chronicles of Narnia*, or *The Lord of the Rings*. The Egyptians, for example, represented Seti, god of darkness, as a hippopotamus, and Canaanite myth often depicted the god of death skulking in swamps. The *Gilgamesh* epic has a bull as its central character.

Perhaps the point of this passage is to further elucidate the point made in chapters 38 and 39. God and his ways are unknowable. What better way to reinforce that truth by asking the question: 'Did you ever ask yourself why God made the hippopotamus? Or the whale?' The answer, of course, is that we have no idea. And pain is like that! We don't understand it! But it is not important that *we* understand it; what is important for us to know is that *God* understands it!

It may be that this section is reinforcing the idea that much of God's providence is *incomprehensible* to us. *To us — not to God!*

We are to live with mystery every day of our lives, just as we will in heaven. Even there, in heaven, there will be things that will baffle us, confound us, knock us off our feet. With angels, we will be in awe of the complexity of what God does.

But there will never be a moment when we shall conclude: this isn't fair. Never!

The truth encapsulated in Romans 8:28, that everything works out in fulfilment of a divine and all-wise plan, does not imply that we can fathom its intricate blueprints. Sometimes all we can do is gasp at its audacity and sublimity. God's providence takes our breath away.

But perhaps there is more here than that. This point, after all, had been the message of chapters 38 and 39 as God had asked Job to survey the universe and ponder its complexity and intricacy. Here, in chapters 40 and 41, God is saying something more. Leviathan and Behemoth are representatives of evil, *of Satan*! Job, remember, knew virtually nothing about Satan. He was certainly entirely ignorant of the first two chapters where we are told of Satan's wager: 'allow me to take away from Job all that he has and you will see him in full scale denial'. That, mercifully, had proved to be false. But Job had come very close to it, blaming God for what in fact had been Satan's doing. Now he is being told in the language of pictures that another *being* is at work in the universe. This creature is powerful and threatening. And fearsome! 'He is king over all the sons of pride' (41:34).

Is this what Job confesses following the depictions of these two beasts, when he says, 'I had heard of you by the hearing of the ear, but now my eye sees you' (42:5)? Has Job come to realize that God is so powerful that not even the threats of

Satan himself can undo his purpose towards his own? Satan may well be uncontrollable as far as we are concerned:

'Will you play with him as with a bird,
    or will you put him on a leash for your girls?'

(41:5).

But he is not uncontrollable as far as God is concerned. Job may not be able to overcome Leviathan's power. He may not be able to 'draw out Leviathan with a fishhook or press down his tongue with a cord', or 'put a rope in his nose or pierce his jaw with a hook' (41:1-2).

But *God can*! That is what Job has come to see. No matter how evil things may appear, or how afraid he may be, God is in control of everything and nothing is a threat to him. To express it in New Testament terms: 'in all these things we are more than conquerors through him who loved us. For I am sure that neither death nor life, nor angels nor rulers, nor things present nor things to come, nor powers, nor height nor depth, nor anything else in all creation, will be able to separate us from the love of God in Christ Jesus our Lord' (Rom. 8:37-39). He who is able to 'seize the dragon' (Rev. 20:2), the 'great dragon … the deceiver of the whole world' (Rev. 12:9), will be victorious. How come? 'The reason the Son of God appeared was to destroy the works of the devil' (1 John 3:8).

There is no power that can undo the purposes of Almighty God. Job finds himself reduced to confessing his ignorance *and* his sinfulness:

'I know that you can do all things;
    no plan of yours can be thwarted…
Surely I spoke of things I did not understand,

things too wonderful for me to know…
My ears had heard of you
    but now my eyes have seen you.
Therefore I despise myself
    and repent in dust and ashes'

(42:2, 3, 5, NIV).

Job had failed to consider the complexity of God's ways. He had also failed to consider the malevolence of Satan. Who can fathom how God 'allows sin and evil', but yet is not the author of it? Who of us can understand how God can bring Satan into the picture as he does in the opening chapters, saying to him, 'Have you considered my servant Job?' while at the same time maintaining his own moral goodness and perfection.

The devil wants us to think about him as little as possible. He is never happier than when he is ignored. As Lewis so cleverly put it:

> …the more a man was in the Devil's power, the less he would be aware of it, on the principle that a man is still fairly sober as long as he knows he's drunk. It is the people who are fully awake and trying hard to be good who would be most aware of the Devil. It is when you start arming against Hitler that you first realize your country is full of Nazi agents. Of course, they don't want you to believe in the Devil. If devils exist, their first aim is to give you an anaesthetic — to put you off your guard. Only if that fails, do you become aware of them.[3]

For a while, a good while, the devil had gained a victory over Job. But now the anaesthetic has worn off. His mask has fallen. Job has come to see that the universe is much more complicated than he had first assumed.

But God is still in control. And that is the best instruction he can receive. The shadow of the cross falls over every Christian's pain and says, 'That pain is mine.' 'I am filling up what is lacking in Christ's afflictions' (Col. 1:24). And what is more wondrous still, God has sent his Son into the world so that in his life and death, he has 'disarmed the rulers and authorities and put them to open shame, by triumphing over them in him' (Col. 2:15).

Job has only glimpsed it, of course. Like a man who desires to see over a wall, jumps into the air to catch a fleeting glimpse of what lies the other side, so Job has caught a moment's glance at what lies 'the other side' of the cross. He has caught sight of the victory — a victory which he cannot fully explain, but which he knows to be a certainty.

It is something that holds true for every believer. For you and for me.

For your journal...

1. We mentioned the possibility that Behemoth and Leviathan might be symbols for Satan. Meditate on the words of Peter: 'Be sober-minded; be watchful. Your adversary the devil prowls around like a roaring lion, seeking someone to devour' (1 Peter 5:8).

2. In what ways was Job 'repenting' in 42:6?

Day 27
Hope returns

Job 42

*'And the L*ORD *restored the fortunes of Job,*
when he had prayed for his friends.
*And the L*ORD *gave Job twice as much*
as he had before'
(Job 42:10).

Suggested reading: Job 42:1-11

And they all lived happily ever after! Unexpected as it is, the book of Job really does end this way. Gone are the days of darkness and gloom. Spring has arrived. God's favour returns. His face shines on Job once more. Are the memories of Job's pain erased? No! But they are built upon so as to make the past a little less painful than it has been.

Time heals, they say. Actually, it isn't time so much as God's presence that heals. Knowing that he is there — *here!* — makes all the difference.

> Even though I walk
>   through the valley of the shadow of death,
>   I will fear no evil,
> for you are with me…

(Ps. 23:4).

God is speaking to Job at last! And yes, the lessons Job has been learning have been painful, and bewildering. But at least God is present! The silence has been deafening, but the voice of the Lord has brought a calm and serenity to the situation. God may well be angry with Job's friends, because they 'have not spoken of me what is right' (42:7, 8 *twice*). But not with Job. There is a relationship that Job has with God that is summed up in the phrase 'my servant' (42:7-8, *four times*; cf. 1:8). It is an expression that the Scriptures use of men like Moses and David (Num. 12:7; 2 Sam. 7:5). It is also the way God speaks about Jesus in the Servant Songs of Isaiah (Isa. 42:1; 52:13; 53:11). It is almost as though God is singling Job out and saying to him, 'You are special to me!'

God's grace always does that! It singles us out and confers upon us favour that we do not expect or deserve.

'The LORD made [Job] prosperous again...' (42:10, NIV). Amazing grace...! But what about those lessons? What exactly did Job learn?

- Trials may come when we least expect them. They often come unannounced and without anticipation. Things may be fine one day and terrible the next. 'Accidents' happen without a moment's notice. We are rarely given an opportunity to prepare ourselves for what may lie ahead.

- There is no limit to the severity of a trial we may be asked to endure, other than the promise that it will not be 'beyond your ability' (1 Cor. 10:13). There are no areas of life from which we are exempt being tested simply because we are Christians. We cannot say of a particular hurt, 'A

Christian would never experience that!' AIDS, the loss of a family member through suicide, multiple deformity, paraplegia, psychosis… we are not exempt from any of these simply because we are believers.

• We can never say about a trial, 'God isn't in this!' Such analysis is out of joint. It belittles God's sovereignty, reducing him to an 'extra' in the unfolding of our lives. If God isn't sovereign, then he isn't God! Here, in the suffering of Job, God is just as much 'at work' as anywhere else in Job's life. The conclusion to the book of Job speaks of family members and friends consoling Job 'over all the trouble the LORD had brought upon him' (42:11, NIV). When bad things happen, God is right there in the very centre of things.

• Satan is more malevolent, more cunning, more petulant than we ever think. Hard as it is to think of a creature who is 'pure evil', Satan is one. There are no limits to his schemes. His aim is to bring as much dishonour to God and those who belong to God as he can. His unimaginable malice, fury and cruelty against everything that is God's takes a variety of forms; but principally, he is cunning, often beyond our capacity to discern. He makes evil appear as good and good as evil, twisting everything in his mind and ours (2 Cor. 11:14). Not taking him seriously can be our downfall. He is never happier than when he is ignored, for it is then that we often mistake his work for God's. When we blame God for actions that are Satan's, he is ecstatic.

• Our best friends may prove to be a disappointment when things get really tough. The counselling techniques of Job's friends had proved fatally flawed. They made categorical errors of fact and judgement. Their insistence that suffering is always divine punishment was both annoying and erroneous. Though Job himself was responsible for his lapse in responding to their insensitive assertions, that did not make their remarks any less erroneous.

- Additionally, to suggest that all suffering is the direct consequence of a particular sin on our part is unwise, unhelpful and incorrect. Instant retribution does happen on occasions, in that sometimes God will judge sin straight away. But it was not so in this case.

- Some trials do not go away quickly. Prayer is always the first resort, but sometimes it will not remove the trial. Just as Paul had to learn to live with a thorn in the flesh, that submission did not come to him quickly (2 Cor. 12:7-10). It came following his instinctive desire for its removal. Much needless pain is added when we suggest that it is the essence of saintliness to acquiesce to pain without any reluctance on our part. Job's initial responses in chapters 1 and 2 are astonishing, but we are also to learn that his later questioning is not necessarily something about which God disapproves. Job erred, it is true. But his error was not in the fact that he had trouble accepting the future as he saw it. Jesus teaches us in the Garden of Gethsemane that it is part of the human psyche to shrink from what appears painful and debilitating.

- And some trials do not go away at all. The loss of Job's children was something Job would live with for the rest of his life. The pain grew less as time passed, and as God's grace enabled him to focus on other things; but, it is bad counselling, and poor pastoral care, to make light of the pain of personal bereavement. Christians grieve, too!

- Providence is always purposive. It is always intelligent rather than whimsical. There is a reason for everything — *everything*! We may not be able to detect what that reason is; in fact, more often than not, the purpose may be incomprehensible to us. It may be like the hippopotamus! The reason for its existence may be beyond our capacity to discern, but it is not beyond God's. However mysterious things may be to us, they are not so to God. Even if God chose to disclose that purpose, it is doubtful that we could ever understand it. But it is not important that we understand it; it is only important that *he* does.

- The purposes of God in suffering are designed specifically for each individual. God treated Job severely because he wanted Job to be more useful to him. After all, we still talk about Job! And study his life! Those whom God intends to use most significantly, he often treats with particular care. The training for those who are to be placed in the front line of battle is all the more intensive and painstaking. It is not necessarily a pronounced perverseness that is the reason why some battle with hardships all of their lives; rather, it is because God has intentions for special service which will require skills learned in battle. Those who are called to follow the King most closely need not wonder if they, too, become targets for the enemy's fire. Pain thus becomes a training ground for further usefulness.

- Trials are dangerous times for our souls. Job has said things which he ought never to have said. He has discredited God's justice (40:8). He has spoken words 'without knowledge' (38:2). Trials, as the book of Hebrews reminds, can sometimes embitter (Heb. 12:15). Trials do not contain within themselves the guarantee of spiritual benefit. Our response to them is crucial. Watchfulness and prayerfulness are the keys to ensuring a good outcome. Of the three on the crosses at Calvary, one atoned, another was sanctified, and, just as surely, the third hardened. Nor was Job's initial good response a guarantee against future lapses. Some sins take time to root. Constant vigilance is required.

These are some of the lessons that Job has unfolded for us. Perhaps you have learned different lessons. Make sure you record them and remember them often.

For your journal...

1. In this chapter we mentioned many lessons that Job may well have learned. Can you think of some others?

2. What lessons have you learned in the course of this study on Job? Take some time to write them down and pray over each one.

Day 28
'Happily ever after'

Job 42:7-17

*'And the LORD blessed the latter days of Job
more than his beginning'
(Job 42:12).*

Suggested reading: Job 42:12-17

One lesson, however, remains. It is the one recounted in the beautiful tale that brings this book to a close. It would be difficult to think of a better ending than this one. Job is not only restored to his former prosperity; he is given 'twice as much as he had before' (42:10). There are pictures of family gatherings, friends who gather for a meal, gifts and kind words spoken by those who love him (42:11). His livestock — sheep, camels, oxen, donkeys — are numbered as double what he had possessed before the trial (42:12; cf. 1:3).

And children! Seven sons and three girls. The girl's names are delightful, reflecting something of the joy they must have brought him: *Jemimah* meaning 'a dove', *Keziah* meaning 'cinnamon', and *Keren-Happuch* meaning 'container of antimony' — a highly prized eye shadow (42:14).

Can't you imagine Job pouring out his love for these children? Did that mean he had forgotten all about his past? No,

of course not. Pain like that does not simply vanish. But good
things can come to help refocus and restore. Spring arrives.

As Joni Eareckson Tada puts it:

God's pruning shears seem merciless. Nothing escapes
the cutting edge of His will. Not the blossom of youth,
not the bloom of good health, not the fruit of prosperity, not the sturdy, growing family. None of these fall
outside the pruning effects of God's purposes.

But spring comes, doesn't it? Much to our amaze-
ment, it even came to Job. A spring of such fragrance
and beauty that his long, bitter winter must have seemed
like a bad dream…

Hope returns. New life pokes up from the dead stump.
Joy reappears … ever so slowly, almost shyly, and not all
at once. But it comes. Fresh new grace enables us to
endure. Bright, hopeful promises offer a strong trellis to
which we can cling. The sweet fragrance of the Holy
Spirit blows across our lives, waters us with His word,
and encourages us to reach for all the good things God
has in store for us.

In God's order, winter always gives way to spring. The
iron grip of January yields to the sunshine of His love. If
not now, then soon.

Spring will not tarry. New life is on the way.[1]

The trouble with some pains is that they stick to us like
superglue. We find ourselves unable to get beyond the pain.
We seem stuck, as it were, crippled by its tortuous character.
In our western cultures, despite the trappings of solidarity, the
grieving process, like so much else, takes place in seclusion.
Days when folk appear happy and content are masks for

tortured hours spent alone with one's thoughts (nightmares!), trapped by something that will not let us go. The pitfalls have been noted: a fixation on the events that have occurred, re- living the episode over and over so that it takes on a life of its own. Then comes depression, the thought that we can never be happy again, that life is permanently scarred from now on and nothing can change that state of affairs. Then comes the most serious condition of all, perhaps: the internalization of grief. As J. I. Packer expresses it:

> This is a condition of denial in which an unfulfilled spirit of mourning, driven deep and still hurting subliminally, sours our conscious life with bitterness, cynicism, ap- athy, cosmic resentment, and unforgiveness of any who in any way seem to have contributed to the loved one's death.[2]

What we find in these closing lines, 'happily-ever-after'- style though they appear to be, is a story of how God unravels Job's twisted soul. Now that the lesson of his sovereignty has been learned (could Job have learned it any other way?), God restores him in a way that displays his love for Job. And in response, a forgiven Job shows forgiveness to his insensitive friends. All traces of bitterness are gone from Job's heart. He acts as priest (he lived before priests were institutionalized within Israel), and the friends bring bulls and rams in abun- dance as a burnt offering (42:8). Job's prayer on their behalf is heard, and the friends are spared the indignation that they deserved (42:9).

Life can change! What seems like an endless winter can change into spring again. Hope returns. Life is filled with meaning and purpose again. The sounds of singing and

laughter are heard without the accompanying guilt that somehow this isn't right. Why else would the book of Job record
the words: 'And in all the land there were no women so beautiful as Job's daughters' (42:15)?

There is no guarantee, this side of eternity, that Job's pattern
will be anyone else's. Some are asked to carry their sorrows to
the grave (but no further than the grave!). Yet for many the
demands are less arduous. God steps in and changes things.
Life becomes bearable again. Perspectives shift.

Job lives to be an old man — 140 years, the age of many of
the patriarchs (42:16). Did he never think again about the
ten children that he lost? Of course he did! Probably every
day! But they were 'quiet thoughts' — thoughts that rest content in the knowledge that God had a purpose in it all that he
could not comprehend.

They were submissive thoughts; thoughts interrupted by
the sound of other children playing at his feet.

If joy is, as C. S. Lewis suggests, 'the serious business of
heaven', then what Job receives is a little foretaste of heaven
here on earth. It is not heaven itself, of course, for this world
is upside down. But it is a foretaste, and the last verse, which
speaks of Job's death, is, for Job, only the beginning of an eternity with God.

Does Job understand now the reasons for his trials? Not
entirely. He knows that it has been for his benefit. He rests in
the certainty that he has not been the victim of whim or
caprice.

But there are areas, too, that remain a mystery to him. There
are things he does *not* know. Knowing them would make him
as knowledgeable and as wise as God himself.

Job must live with mystery in heaven, too, as we all will
have to. There will be no doubting God's benevolence or

integrity in choosing the path he has for each one of us. There will be worship in the face of an infinite wisdom at work in our lives.

But there will be mystery, too.

When life hurts, the most wise persons settle for not knowing, and not even trying to guess, the details of God's intricate plan and purpose.

'Oh, the depth of the riches and wisdom and knowledge of God! How unsearchable are his judgements and how inscrutable his ways!'

(Rom. 11:33).

That is still Job's song, even today. Is it yours?

For your journal...

1. It has been twenty-eight days since we began this study (if you followed the course as intended, that is!). It is time to reflect on what you may have learned from the book of Job. What expectations did you have at the beginning of the study that weren't fulfilled? Were there any surprises?

2. What issues remain unresolved in your mind as you come to the end of this book? How will you deal with them?

Notes

Preface

1. *Making the Most of Your Devotional Life*, Auburn, MA/ Darlington, England, 2001, p.20.

Day 1: Give me wisdom

1. C. S. Lewis, *A Grief Observed*, Seabury Press, New York, 1961, p.27.

Day 3: 'The prince of darkness'

1. John Calvin, *The Institutes of the Christian Religion*, ed. John T. McNeill, 2 vols., trans. Ford Lewis Battles, I. xviii.1, The Westminster Press, Philadelphia, 1975, 1:230.

Day 4: The sovereignty of God

1. *Westminster Confession of Faith* 3.1.
2. James I. Robertson Jr, *Stonewall Jackson: The Man, The Soldier, The Legend*, Macmillan Publishers USA, New York, 1997, pp.158-9.

Day 7: Singing the blues

1. Joni Eareckson Tada, *Secret Strength*, Scripture Press, Amersham-on-the-hill, Bucks, 1989, pp.170-1.
2. B. B. Warfield, 'The Emotional Life of our Lord', in *The Person and Work of Christ*, Presbyterian and Reformed Publishing Co., Nutley, N. J., 1970, pp.132-3.

Day 8: The failure of counselling
1. John Calvin, *Sermons on Job*, facsimile edition of the 1574 edition, Sermon 62 (on Job 16:1-9), Banner of Truth, Edinburgh, 1993, p.290.

Day 10: Looking for an arbitrator
1. *The Message: Job*, by Eugene Peterson, NavPress, Colorado Springs, CO, 1996, p.31.

Day 11: In the dark
1. Peterson, *The Message*, pp.32-3.

Day 14: My Redeemer lives
1. Robert Davis, *My Journey into Alzheimer's Disease*, Tyndale Press, USA, 1993, pp.22-3.

Day 17: Justice denied
1. C. S. Lewis, *Reflections on the Psalms.*
2. Calvin Beisner, *Psalms of promise*, Presbyterian and Reformed, Grand Rapids: MI, 1994 (1988), pp.165-83.
3. John Calvin, *Commentary on the Psalms,* The Calvin Translation Society, Grand Rapids, MI: Baker Book House, 1979, 2:404.

Day 18: Mining for wisdom
1. Isaac Watts' rendition of Psalm 147, 'Praise ye the Lord, tis good to raise…'.
2. From *Hesperides: To the Virgins, to make much of Time.*

Day 19: The fear of God
1. Hilary of Poitiers, *De Trinitate* I. xviii. Cf. Calvin: 'God alone is a fit witness of himself in his Word'. John Calvin, *The Institutes of the Christian Religion*, I. vii. 4, 1:79.

2. Sinclair Ferguson, *The Pundit's Folly,* The Banner of Truth, Edinburgh, 1995, p.74.

Day 24: Questions, questions and more questions

1. William Henry Green, *Conflict and Triumph: The Argument of the Book of Job Unfolded,* The Banner of Truth, Edinburgh, 1999, p.138.
2. Herman Bavinck, *The Doctrine of God,* Baker, Grand Rapids, MI, 1977 (1951), p.13.
3. Helen Roseveare, testifying to God's grace following her five-month abduction and rape when a missionary in Congo/Zaire in 1964, in *He Gave Us a Valley,* Inter-Varsity Press, 1976, pp.180-1.

Day 25: Dungeons and dragons

1. C. S. Lewis, *A Grief Observed* , Bantam, New York, 1976, p.81.

Day 26: The faint glimmer of comprehension

1. See Henry M. Morris, *The Remarkable Record of Job,* Baker Book House, Grand Rapids, MI, 1988, pp.115-7. Since, according to this view, the dinosaur became extinct before the Flood, the view also necessitates that Job lived *before* Noah. Others have placed Job in a later period making this view untenable.
2. Morris contends that such creatures could well have existed, giving rise to the folk-lore about fire-breathing dragons.
3. C. S. Lewis, *God in the Dock: Essays on Theology and Ethics.* Edited by Walter Hooper, Eerdmans, Grand Rapids, MI, 1970, pp.56-7.

Day 28: 'Happily ever after'

1. Joni Eareckson Tada, *Secret Strength,* pp.76-7.
2. J. I. Packer, *A Grief Sanctified,* p.165.

A wide range of excellent books on spiritual subjects is available from Evangelical Press. Please write to us for your free catalogue or contact us by e-mail.

Evangelical Press
Faverdale North Industrial Estate, Darlington, DL3 0PH, England

Evangelical Press USA
P. O. Box 84, Auburn, MA 01501, USA

e-mail: sales@evangelicalpress.org

web: www.evangelicalpress.org